Christian Logic 3

WAS JESUS A MYTH?

Dr. Thomas Childs

www.thomaschilds.net

Book Layout ©2017 BookDesignTemplates.com

Ordering Information:

Quantity sales. Special discounts are available on quantity purchases by corporations, associations, and others. For details, contact the "Special Sales Department" at the address above.

Book Title/ Author Name. —1st ed.

ISBN: 978-1985575943

Contents

I dedicate this book to all my friends who have trusted me with their questions about faith and helped me rediscover the joy of finding answers to the understanding we seek.

"Jerry, just remember, it's not a lie, if you believe it."

—George Costanza (Seinfeld)

INTRODUCTION

Was Jesus a Myth?

"And the day will come when the mystical generation of Jesus, by the supreme being as his father in the womb of a virgin will be classed with the fable of the generation of Minerva in the brain of Jupiter. But we may hope that the dawn of reason and freedom of thought in these United States will do away all this artificial scaffolding..." - Thomas Jefferson, Letters of Thomas Jefferson (Letter to John Adams, April 11, 1823)

It has long been predicted that people would eventually explain away the person of Jesus Christ as little more than a mythological figure. From what I am personally seeing, I feel this day has arrived. And I am not simply talking about skeptics. More and more, my conversations with curious people seeking answers about God or Christianity begin not with questions about scriptures, practices, or teachings from Jesus Christ. Instead, the dialogue almost always starts with unanswered questions that have become roadblocks to even considering Jesus Christ or Christianity in the first place.

And indeed, there are many, many questions. Questions about hypocritical Christians. Questions about the institutional church. Questions about other world religions. Questions about heaven and, dare I say it, hell. Questions about *PBS* and *Discovery Channel* specials on religion. Questions about aliens and life on other planets. Questions about science and God. Questions about dinosaurs, the Big Bang, Evolution, and so much more. At first glance, you might think there is an infinite amount of questions with infinite possibilities for answers. It can be overwhelming.

In truth however, I have observed that there are *not* an infinite amount of questions that people ask when it comes to God, faith, and potential roadblocks to faith. In fact, as I enter my third decade of working with people to answer their various questions, what I am seeing is that, while we each individually feel our questions and roadblocks to faith are unique, in actuality, we are asking the same questions so many others are asking and have asked for centuries. Sure, our modern-day questions are dressed in new clothes of modern technology and current trends, but the gist of our concerns invariably harken back to what has stumped others in the past and present. You are not alone in your questions about God and faith. More to the point, there is a 99.99% chance that countless others have struggled with the same questions, concerns, and issues that you wrestle with.

I have written this *Christian Logic* series to address the most prevalent, most often asked and frequently visited questions that people have and continue to bring to me regarding their initial struggles with faith in God. And, these are foundational questions that *everyone* ought to be able to answer, regardless of whether you believe in God or not. The reason is because, without answers to these questions, most of us would not have a balanced view of God, much less Jesus Christ or any semblance of authentic spirituality. In *Christian Logic 1* and *Christian Logic 2,* my goal was to provide a starting point for finding answers regarding God, science, and the general tenets of Christianity.

In this book, *Christian Logic 3,* my goal is to address even more questions, only this time I want to address the very specific historical person of Jesus Christ. In this, we will look at questions like: Was Jesus a real, historical person? What is the evidence for Jesus being a historical person? Was the crucifixion of Jesus real? Is there logical evidence to believe in the resurrection? Why does the resurrection really matter anyway? Isn't it enough just to believe Jesus was a historical person and to follow his moral and ethical teachings? And more.

Great questions. And while some people might shy away from these and other similar questions for a variety of reasons, I want to take the opposite approach. I say, "Embrace your questions!" Use your brain. Seek answers. For it is in the discovery of answers that true faith is formed. The only type of belief that transforms us is a personal faith that is developed through self-discovery and logical, common sense thinking. Yes, we need to sometimes "just believe," and we often need the help of other people to guide us on our journey of faith. But never can or should someone else learn something for you, have faith for you, or tell you what your faith ought to be. Whenever that happens, your faith will be powerless when the storms come. And come they will, it's just a matter of time.

So my hope for you, the reader, is this: Ask. Seek. And stop allowing unanswered questions determine whether you will have a meaningful faith in God and Jesus Christ, or not. Even more, I hope you will not let your negative experiences of faith in the past undermine your quest to have a better life, which, I believe, God can fundamentally help you find. Where faith is concerned, we always, always have the possibility for a better *today,* because faith teaches that indeed, we can *fix ourselves* today. Peace can be had today. Joy, hope, contentment, and love can be had today. And it is not about what all those other people are doing. It is never about someone else's story. All that matters is *your* story, and your ability to find peace and abundance in your own heart and life. Finding answers to life's most challenging questions are a foundational part of discovering transformation in our own stories. As such, where your story is concerned, ask your questions, seek answers, and with an open mind, God promises you will find the answers you seek. My hope is that these books will provide at least a stepping-stone for that process to happen.

I might add one other point: in your journey, if you find that God, if Jesus Christ, does not stand up to your scrutiny, then at least you know the facts. You learned for yourself the answers to your questions. And, you can move along in life with a clear conscience, knowing that you did all in your power to truly understand God and how faith in God might matter. On the other hand, if you ask questions, seek answers, and *find* answers, here is what I know: Your life will be transformed, for the better, forever. I say that because *my* life has been transformed for the better forever. And this happened for me, in no small way, because I have spent a good portion of my life asking questions, seeking answers, and *actually finding them.*

It is an amazing thing when "the light bulb" goes off concerning God and faith. I truly hope that happens for you through the reading of these materials.

More to the point, I hope the time you spend working through these questions helps you to see, at least a little, both how real God is and how much he loves you. Good stuff.

CHAPTER 1

The Problem with Truth

"It's a wonder of human behavior: we build
our own handcuffs that trap and harm us.
We create the myth, and we honor it.
We tell the lie, and we believe it."
— *Raif Badawi, 1000 Lashes: Because I Say What I Think*

George Costanza (*Seinfeld*) once advised, "Jerry, just remember, it's not a lie, if you believe it." And the audience laughs hysterically. But deep down, I wonder how many of us think this might actually be true? If a person 100%, absolutely believes something, is it really a lie? Can a person believe anything they wish, and be telling the truth, if only they are sincere? The obvious answer is no, but I would suggest to you that *everyone* to one extent or another believes in things that are neither true nor right, yet in our sincerity, we are utterly convinced that what we believe is the "truth." This is a serious problem with "truth."

My opening question: *should logic, truth and facts* matter concerning our conversations about spirituality, God, or especially Jesus Christ? Or in reality, is there no such thing as truth, real facts, or logic where God and spirituality are concerned? Can anyone believe anything they want to believe about God, no matter how contradictory, and still be right? Should "logic" and "right" even be in a conversation regarding faith, given that so many people feel that we can believe anything we wish, and everyone be right?

I will attempt to answer that question fairly clearly in the upcoming pages, but as an introduction, I simply point the idea that no one really believes in competing truth. In the guise of inclusiveness and being nice, we claim that anyone can believe anything they wish, just so long as we can all just get along with one another. But underneath the desire for us all to get along, the reality is that no one really believes in alternative truth or alternative facts. Why? It is simply because alternative facts do not exist. Alternative truth in and of itself does not and cannot exist. That being said, you can believe that someone else disagrees with you, and they have the potential to be right. But, the moment you actually *believe* that they are right is the very moment you change your own beliefs. In this, you have the truth. You have the facts. Then you have everything else.

2 + 2 = 4. Yes? There is truth and fact, then there is everything else. And while some may say this applies to math or science but not religion, I would argue that it is the same in every single area of life, including religion. Just as there is a correct equation for math facts, there also is a correct equation for religion and faith. All religious beliefs are not true and cannot be true, because many of them very clearly contradict each other. All religious claims about spirituality and faith are not good. Doubt that, and simply explain to me how the ISIS religious fanatics who behead infidels or suicide bombers who terrorize mothers and children in a public marketplace are right and true and good in their

actions? Or, listen to any of the recent Hollywood interviews of scientology devotees who have recently disavowed their faith and made fairly serious (and terrible) accusations against the scientology movement. The point is: many of these religious perspectives are not only wrong, they are sick, and no "logical" person would question it.

Why does this matter? It's because, with any amount of attention to the details, any thinking person must ultimately come to a point where we realize that all religions are not the same, some are more right and true than others, and some are far, far more destructive than others. They cannot all be right. They cannot all be good, and they cannot all be true. There are simply no alternative truths *anywhere* in life. There is truth, then there is everything else, and this most certainly applies to religion and spirituality. The bottom line here is, "Of course logic, truth, and the facts matter. Of course, it matters if what you believe is wrong, regardless of how sincere or convinced you or I may be."

Which brings me to the point of this particular book, *Christian Logic 3.* In my previous two books, I have argued that there indeed are *facts* that lead any thinking person directly to the unavoidable and incontrovertible conclusion that God exists. Even more, our ability to think, to reason, to discover facts and truth, to use logic and the scientific method all lead us *to* believe in God, not the opposite.

Christian. Facts. Christian. Logic. Two seemingly independent topics that many say have no place in the same sentence, much less conversation. Spirituality. Facts. Truth. Logic. These are topics that a host of people find irreconcilably different and full of contradictions, yet when it comes to our personal beliefs, we often don't see the problem with living in such contradictions. When we do this, our views of life, philosophy, religion and certainly God are often ripe with problems, potholes, paradox, unabashed prejudice and willful ignorance, but we often

7

think it doesn't matter. But it *does* matter. In fact, it matters for each and every one of us more than anything else in the world. Why? Because prisoners go to prison precisely because they don't live within the rules. And it doesn't matter if they "knew" the rules when they broke them. Life itself has rules. There are rules to finding peace in life. There are rules to what makes a marriage work. There are rules to raising good kids. There are rules for overcoming anxiety, depression, fear, or finding victory in pretty much any situation. There are rules that keep a society from devolving into chaos. And all of these rules are grounded in truth and the truth about correct thinking, living and behavior.

If we want to live authentically free and abundant lives, we must both know and embrace the rules, and thus the truth, that lead to our best life possible. Along this journey, only the truth will set you free. It is no good to keep thinking any path will lead to life and life in abundance, just as it is no good to think you can live however you want in society and not get in trouble with the police or even go to jail. *It is ironic yet inherently true that the rule followers in life are the ones with the most freedom.* This most certainly applies to our spiritual and emotional freedom.

Regarding the most profound freedom (emotional and spiritual) life has to offer, it is critical to understand that only truth (not alternative truth) will answer the most important questions about why we are here, what we are supposed to be doing with our lives, where we are headed, and how we will find peace, love, hope, contentment and joy along the way. Only truth leads to life. But, it is *such* a struggle to discover this truth because there are so many competing, even contradictory, voices teaching us that *their* way is the best, perhaps even the only way to find what we seek. And I am not simply talking about teachings or leaders that we encounter in life. I also am talking about what we learn from our experiences as well. As we grow up, each voice sways us a little this way, other voices pull in that direction. And it is not uncommon to start believing a bit of *all* of them, even if they are incompatible. and leading us to our own misery.

In this, a huge sign of personal maturity and growth is when a person begins to realize (to become self-aware) that, especially where spirituality and God are concerned, all the voices we hear cannot possibly be right. It is also no small thing to realize that, when compiling our own definitions of "good, right and true," there is no such thing as alternative facts or competing truths. Everything we have learned about God, faith, and spirituality cannot possibly right or true, and yet often we don't realize our own inner inconsistencies. With spirituality, just as in math and science, there is truth. There is fact. Then there is everything else.

At my church, *LifePoint,* we like the phrase, "Use Your Brain." The idea is that each and every one of us must remember that God gave us brains for the very purpose of using those brains to discover *truth.* Not alternative truth, and not competing truth. No, *the* truth. The truth about what? Well, whatever and wherever it is that we are searching for answers. One reason is because, *just as wrong medications do not lead to healing, so also wrong answers to life's questions do not lead to solutions.* Why? Because it is only through correct diagnosis of a problem that healing can be found. It is only in *thinking that is grounded in truth* that life is transformed. It is only through *truth* that our deepest, ultimate questions and problems will ever find answers and resolution. However, the *challenge* is to actually allow our brains the option to engage the discovery process, rather than shutting down the process before it really ever begins. We do this so quickly and easily by simply assuming we already know all we need to know, regardless of how wrong our knowledge may be. Why do I say that?

Well, think of your own story. Where in your past has a negative experience regarding God, faith, hypocritical Christians, getting burned or burned out trying to "do the right thing" led you to a time of disillusionment regarding God or the importance of spirituality? When did God not do what you wanted? When did any other disappointing life experience cause you to "lose your faith?" When did a Christian *person* darken your heart towards Christian *teachings?* We all have those stories. We all have those seasons of disappointment and disillusionment. The common response often is to say, "If God is like *that,* then .... " We all fill in the blank in different ways, yet the end result is the same. We walk away. The thing is though, what if God is *not* like that, but we just totally misinterpreted and misunderstood the "truth" of the situation? What if Jesus Christ had absolutely nothing to do with what that "Christian person" did or said to you?

In our bad experiences, it is very common to believe we learned the truth about God, while at the same time never questioning ourselves or other people in the process. Over time, more and more voices add to our perceived, developing truth. And with each new, adopted voice, we develop more and more ammunition to walk away from God or do anything serious with our spirituality or faith. I would submit though, what is happening is *not* that we are discovering and living increasingly into the *real truths* of God and spirituality. Instead, in our minds, we are picking through our life experiences to construct "alternative truths" that justify our decision to walk away from God or a spiritual life, regardless of how illogical, unreasonable, or irrational our arguments may actually be. We sincerely believe in our developing truth. But what I am hoping you will see is that, for all of us, the problem is that our new, "alternative truth" is in point of fact, either very flawed or even no truth at all.

One of the more common ways we develop alternative truth is called circular logic (circular reasoning or circular proving). Circular logic is the idea that A is true because B is true, thus B is true because A is true. Another way to think of this in terms of a "logical fallacy" where, if one or more components of the argument are true, then the conclusion must also be true. Let's make this simple. Take George Costanza's advice as an example, using circular logic like this:

"It is not a lie, if you sincerely believe it."

Therefore:

> If you sincerely believe it, it must be true.
> If it is true, it must be right.
> If it is right, it must be good.
> If it is good, it must be good for me.
> If it is good for me, then it cannot be a lie.

Ah yes, that sounds so good, so reasonable, so *true*. And, it feels right. The only problem? The entire equation is rubbish, total nonsense. Why? Because A is not true because B is true, nor can you mix and match A, B, E, G and come out with anything that even remotely resembles a correct, logical answer. Regarding our example above, it is not true that, if you are sincere, then you must also be right. It is not true, that if you believe it, it is good. Plenty of people are sincerely wrong. Plenty of people believe things that are bad, but they think they are good, and the end result is neither good for them nor right for anyone. If you want confirmation about what I am saying, consider the ISIS caliphate or any suicide bomber. I am fairly certain a suicide bomber is sincere in what they believe. I am also fairly certainly they think they believe in truth. I also am pretty sure that they believe what they believe is right and good (even if, more for the cause than for themselves), even to the point of death. Even so, if a suicide bomber blew up you, your spouse, kids or family, would you also not argue that any such suicide bomber would be sincerely wrong, and their thinking, methods, and end results are neither good, true, nor right?

Let's add another layer to this developing equation. Confirmation bias. Confirmation bias is a pattern of interpreting data, life events or experiences where individuals proactively seek and sift information that only confirms what they already believe to be true. The most obvious example of confirmation bias is when we choose our "news" channel. We all know how this works. You consider CNN, Fox News, MSNBC, Huffington Post, and so many others. I would suggest that the initial goal of this channel surfing is *not* to find the source that is reporting the news story in the most authentic, unbiased way possible. Instead, the goal is to find whatever channel it is that will report the news the way "I already believe" it ought to be reported. Everyone knows that each news channel has an entirely different version of truth, even though they are reporting the exact same world events. And this is precisely why we scan the channels until we find what we are looking for, notice, *before* the news is ever heard. Talk about confirmation bias. Ouch. The point is that *we all do this,* regardless of what side of the political or societal spectrum you support.

A true sign of maturity is when you can recognize (self-awareness) confirmation bias in your own thought process. To be clear, *everyone* struggles to recognize, much less overcome, confirmation bias. Why? Because we all have flawed, distorted ideas of reality, truth, even of ourselves, that we don't want to challenge, much less change. As such, rather than face our flaws in the mirror, which requires humility and confession (and usually an apology), we choose to make excuses, point fingers of blame, and do whatever possible to "confirm" that whatever we already have done, have believed or will continue to do and believe is right. And with enough effort, we can justify pretty much anything we want to believe. There is a reason the 3 least commonly used words in the English language are, "I am sorry." We could easily add 3 other words to the list, "I was wrong." No one enjoys being "wrong" or "sorry," as it is both humbling and humiliating, it requires self-awareness and transparency, not to mention a host of other qualities, all of which are rarely valued in our culture today.

Where God and spirituality is concerned, these problems are exacerbated because there is no truth, theory, idea or speculation about spirituality or God (or the opposite) that does not also have someone "out there" to validate it. The internet has given us this gift. Want to worship angels? There's a support group for that. Want to worship the stars? There's a support group for that. Want to worship aliens? There's a support group for that. Want to worship Satan? Well, there's a support group for that. Want to oppress your wife? Let me show you both the scriptures and the *people* who believe that is God's will. From killing yourself to murdering other people to abusing yourself to abusing other people, people have used religion, God, the Bible, the Koran, atheism, agnosticism, and every other "ism" to justify believing pretty anything they *already* believed, regardless of how close or far away from the facts and real truth their beliefs may be.

Which brings me back to my previous comments about alternative truth, or alternative facts. Think a moment about these two words, alternative and truth. Or, alternative and facts. The problem with this is that, in its purist form, facts by definition mean offering a perspective that is unbiased, indisputable, clear, and without question. And yet, how often does it happen that people providing their version of "facts" are simply promoting a perspective that may or may not have anything to do with actual reality?

For example, imagine either CNN or Fox News is my trusted source to report the facts. If I watch them long enough, at what point will I start believing what they say is true, for no other reason than I heard it reported from them, and I trust them? I have done no personal investigation. I have not studied the story for myself. I have not looked at the circumstantial evidence. I have not interviewed a witness. I have done almost zero homework. All I know is, "they told me so." What I want to ask in this situation then is, "If the person watching the news sincerely believes the story

they hear, does this then that make the news story *true for them*?"
Catch that? Does the sincerity of the receiver of the news change
the nature of the facts and the truth behind the news story? After
all, if they sincerely believe it, what they believe must be right?
And if it is right, it also must be true? Yes?

Talk about a dilemma when it comes to our conversations
about God. Why? Because everyone, regardless of where you are
on the spectrum of faith, already "believes" something about being
a spiritual person or the nature of God. Even more, literally
everywhere you look, *someone else* already believes whatever it is
that *you* believe, and they are openly teaching it somewhere. To
find their information, we simply watch TV or search the internet,
and presto, our flawed, developing beliefs about God are easily
confirmed. Couple that with what many consider to be the purely
subjective nature of faith, and we have a real problem. Why?
Because this implies everyone can find validation for anything they
want to believe with little more than mouse click or the push of a
remote button.

With this validation, we can move forward in life utterly
convinced that what we believe about God or spirituality is both
right and true. Even worse, it doesn't matter if our ideas are full of
contradictions, logical fallacies, confirmation bias, and paradox,
because spirituality and faith in God is subjective anyway. It is the
idea that we can believe anything we want and still be right. The
bottom line is: where God and spirituality are concerned, all that is
required is to sincerely believe it, and then our beliefs will be true,
no matter if our beliefs are based terribly wrong, full of alternative
truths or false information. In other words, you can believe
anything you want about being a spiritual and good person. And, as
long as you are sincere, your beliefs will be both true and good. Get
that? Sounds like George Costanza doesn't it?

Here is what I know: you already sincerely believe
something about God. It may be that God doesn't exist (atheism).

You may believe God cannot be known (agnosticism). You believe any number of other things too, but the point is that no one comes to a conversation about God without pre-existing beliefs that have been shaped by a myriad of voices from your past. More to the point, no one comes to a conversation about God without sincere beliefs. This is why so many people say, "Never talk about politics or religion at the dinner table!" Why? Because we all believe something, and whatever that something is, we are sincere. When someone else challenges our sincere beliefs, the result is usually an argument, if not worse. The point is to say: No one truly believes in something they already know is wrong or false, no matter how wrong or false their beliefs may actually be.

Which leads to the ultimate issue at hand. For so many people, we believe vastly different things about the nature of God and what constitutes being a good, spiritual person. We cannot all be right. For some, they explain this away with a yawn and a shrug, stating that, since spirituality is subjective, it doesn't matter that our beliefs are contradictory. For others though, the approach of willful ignorance is insufficient. This should and does lead to lots of questions, questions that for the vast majority of people I meet, unfortunately, go completely unanswered. I personally want no part of living with mountains of unanswered questions, nor do I want any part of believing wrong things. I hope you don't either. My rationale is that unanswered questions and wrong thinking never leads to solutions, answers, or holistic living in any area of life.

It is truth that sets us free. It is truth that solves problems. And people who wallow in unanswered questions or in error are inevitably bound to live in a spiritual and emotional pigpen, including continuing problems, frustrations, and challenges that are the natural results of erroneous thinking and flawed logic. It cannot be overstated that the world does not work the way we wish it to be, and no amount of circular, flawed, but sincere beliefs about anything will ever change this fact. There is truth about the way things work, then there is everything else (which is not truth). There is the best path, the right path, then there is everything else. No amount of sincerity will ever change that fact. It is utter nonsense to think that, by being sincere, it makes a person right. It is utter nonsense to think that, by believing it, it also makes what you believe true. It also is utter nonsense to think that if you sincerely believe it, it must be good for you. Truth is good for you. Truth works, not baseless opinion and alternative facts. The *right* way is always the best way, and any path is *not* the correct one. And this certainly applies to our thinking about God and spirituality too.

God is who God is, not who we want Him, believe Him, or disregard Him to be. Just as in math, if 2 + 2 = 4, so also with God, there is right and there is wrong. Because of this, only a right understanding of God will allow us both to know God and experience His abundance and rich blessings in life. Jesus said it best when he told us that only the truth will set a person free. So, let's "Hit the brakes and think for a moment." Use your brain. Where are you getting your information about God? Where are you getting your understandings of truth regarding spirituality? How much of your faith is based on what other people said or did, or a bad experience you may have had, rather than the facts of what you *know* to be true and right through personal investigation and study?

How much of your faith in God and belief in being a "spiritual person" is a result, *not* of actual facts and truth, rather it *is* of simply picking and choosing information to "confirm" the bias you have already had in place for so many years? I get it that a vast majority of people in our world believe they are "spiritual people." However, I am trying to avoid the ridiculous notion that we can all be spiritual people in different ways, and all be right. Again, there are no alternative truths in life. And if we base our life decisions on error and flawed thinking, the results must necessarily be erroneous and flawed. This applies to math. This applies to music. This applies to spirituality, as this applies to God and the person of Jesus Christ too.

Perhaps no person in the history of the human race is more controversial, with more differing opinions and beliefs about Him, than the person of Jesus Christ. I personally believe the primary reason the controversy rages is because so much of what Jesus said and did strikes so close to home for us humans. At the same time though, another reason there is so much controversy is because so, so many people base their beliefs about Jesus, *not* on the facts, but rather on so many other things in life that have little to do with the actual life, teachings, ministry, or facts about Him. As such, most of us already have an opinion about Jesus Christ. Actually, most of us already believe *we know the facts,* about Him.

I would like to suggest that the bulk of what many people claim to be "facts" about Jesus Christ are in reality "alternative truths" that we have selected over time to confirm our preconceived biases about God and spirituality. Past this, all of us, to one extent or another, have engaged confirmation bias to validate our beliefs about God and Jesus Christ, even if we have never truly studied what Jesus taught and lived Himself. And, I include *Christians* in this category. How many Christians believe what they believe about Jesus *not* because they studied the evidence, teachings, life and ministry of Christ on their own, but because they have simply been told something, experienced something, or have a memory of something from parents or a church or whatever else in their past? How many *Christians* consider themselves "spiritual people" even though in truth, all they know is a junior high or high school experience? Yet 10 or 20 or 30 years later, they also think that junior high or high school experience is more than sufficient to tell me what I need to know about church, God and spirituality? Seriously? How does that ever make sense?

Which is where we begin our journey in this book. In this entire *Christian Logic* series, I am hoping we all might stop judging

17

spirituality, the church, the Bible, God, or especially Jesus Christ off some experience you had in the past. Let's lay aside confirmation bias for a moment. Let's set aside logical fallacies, alternative truths, and alternative facts. Instead, with fresh eyes *today*, I hope we can re-engage the person, life and ministry of Jesus Christ with this primary goal: Seek the truth, the *real* truth. Not the truth as someone else told you. Not even the truth as I lay it out in this book. Use your brain. Think for yourself. Learn the arguments for yourself. Study the witnesses for yourself. Examine the evidence. Be constructively critical. Learn the information, then draw your own conclusions.

In this particular book, *Christian Logic 3,* I want to make a case specifically for the person and historicity of Jesus Christ, using clear and concrete evidence, facts, and conclusions based on logic and common sense. I am completely uninteresting in "alternative truths" or "alternative facts" that have been concocted by skeptics who simply have no interest in taking the search for God seriously. I am uninterested in listening to a skeptic ask questions they themselves cannot answer, and then conclude they are smart and right because of it. I also have no interest in offshoot conspiracy theories that are the product of profit-driven authors or doctoral students who have to discover "something new" to get their dissertations approved. Instead, I am sticking with the old cliché, "The easiest, most obvious and logical answer, is more than likely the correct answer." In this, we *should* research, dispute, study, question, and examine the arguments for and against Jesus Christ from every possible angle. However, this is *not* to confirm what we already believe, rather it is to simply learn the truth- the obvious, logical, and most common sense truth that is placed before us. Why? Because it is in the truth, the most logical, common sense and fact-based truth, that transformation is found. It is only in "real truth" that equations are solved and thus transformation and progress is made in life.

To my thesis. There is definitive LOGIC to Christianity and believing in Jesus Christ. If there is *not,* then none of us should believe. Let me say that again: If you study the evidence, and if you come to the conclusion that Jesus, his teachings, life and ministry are either fake or nonsense, then please *do not* believe. You *shouldn't* believe if that is how this plays out. On the other hand, if the evidence leads to an incontrovertible conclusion, then let's put aside this nonsense about "everyone can believe anything they want, and every path, every gate will lead to abundance." No. This is not the way it works in any area of life. So, where Jesus Christ is concerned, study the facts. Learn the arguments, not from the media, or a previous bad experience with God, simplistic personal assumptions, or any other excuse from the past. Instead, setting all of that aside, revisit this idea about God. Revisit the person and life of Jesus Christ. Listen to your questions, seek answers. Ask, *why?* And *using your brain,* allow, of all things, your own personal brain, *your* ability to think, to guide you to true answers that are grounded in evidence and logical thinking.

When it all comes out of the wash, "what other people think" will be completely irrelevant to your own, personal story with God. The only thing that will ultimately matter is your answer to God when He personally asks you, "Who do *you* say that I am?" What is *your* story going to be? To answer that with integrity, we have to study the evidence for ourselves and draw our own conclusions. Do this, and I firmly believe the logic of Christianity becomes the unshakeable foundation upon which we can build everything else that matters, both in this life, and the life to come.

CHAPTER 2

Myths and Superheros

"The great enemy of truth is very often not the lie
(deliberate, contrived and dishonest),
but the myth (persistent, persuasive and unrealistic)."
- John F. Kennedy (Commencement Address at Yale University,
June 11, 1962)

Maybe you have heard the saying, "Never trust a man (or woman) without a limp." What it means is up for debate, but part of the point is to remind us that *everyone* has hurts, pains, scars, mistakes, guilt, "what ifs" and "if onlys" from the past. The problem is that not everyone is willing to admit them. This is the human condition, and it is an unavoidable fact of life. Anyone who acts like they are not fundamentally stricken by this human condition, well, they lie (even if primarily to themselves). Why? Because life is hard. People can be really, really mean. And all of us say and do stupid things, make mistakes, and take intentional and unintentional wrong turns. It continually amazes me how recklessly we live life sometimes (much less hurt each other), with so little thought to both the short and long-term consequences of our thoughts, speech and actions. When those consequences hit, it is beyond ironic that our initial, if not primary, response is to point the finger of blame elsewhere, play the victim, or just sweep the entire conversation under a rug. The result is that we often skid sideways into the future with little to no sense of direction, much less true answers to the problems that never seem to go away or get fixed. Given this, it should come as no surprise that Dr. Phil's most powerful, insightful, and ingenious counseling technique is to simply ask, "How's that working for you?" The evidence is blatantly before us, but we are unwilling to consider it for a variety of reasons.

Where God, much less Jesus Christ, is concerned, perhaps the saying could read, "Never trust a spiritual person without a limp." Why? It is the same principle, only now we apply it to our experiences with God. It is the idea that, you cannot authentically engage God, much less the Christian Gospel, without also being hurt, disillusioned, disappointed, or scarred. And be sure to understand, I am *not* talking about carrying a cross for Christ, or being persecuted because of your faith, or the willingness any of us may have to sacrifice for the greater good. That is a different kind of scar, with a different type of purpose behind it. Instead, what I am talking about are the scars we all bear because of our initial immature, and certainly flawed, experiences with God or Jesus Christ in the past. It could be from a previous experience of God's lack of involvement in our lives (God didn't do what I wanted or expected). It come be from an initial foray into Christianity when a "hypocritical Christian" hurt you or let you down. Either way, the wound was inflicted when God, or Christians, or some *semblance* of a spiritual person hurt or disappointed you deeply. The conclusion we all typically draw? "Well, if God is like *that,* then why should I bother?"

21

To illustrate, I share the testimony of a friend who had what many of us would consider a difficult childhood. For the sake of the illustration, let's call her Lizzy. Lizzy had negligent parents. She experienced abusive language and hateful behaviors in the home. Growing up without the type of unconditional love that every child craves and needs, Lizzy developed co-dependency and self-esteem issues. In the midst of this dysfunctional family environment, if God was ever invoked by the parents, they only talked about God in terms of a multi-syllabic curse word or a yawn. As most children do, there was an initial desire to believe in God, however that soon devolved into unanswered questions and skepticism. These are the same questions (and skepticism) so many of us have when life is unfair: Why would God allow this to happen to me? Why doesn't God do something to fix my situation? If God is like that, and not helping with my suffering, then why would I ever believe in God? Lizzy also tried the church for awhile, only to find she was disappointed with the "hypocritical Christians" she found there, which set the stage for her outright antagonism towards God. Which is exactly what happened.

Moving into adulthood, Lizzy screamed down the road of circular logic and confirmation bias concerning God. Everywhere she looked, mountains of evidence continued to pile up affirming that God is a farce, and anyone who believes in God (much less Jesus Christ) is nothing short of either brainwashed or just outright stupid. All you have to do is look at the news for all the evidence you need. One particular TV evangelist goes to jail for being a liar and a crook. The implication? All Christian leaders, and thus churches, are full of liars and crooks. Another fairly renown Christian is caught in a hotel room with a prostitute and it makes national news. The implication? All Christian leaders, and thus churches, are full of hypocrites who literally tell "us" one thing and then leave that very evening to go "do" another. Another news story cites a church filled with people holding picket signs that read,

"God hates homosexuals." Obviously, God *must* hate homosexuals since those people are holding the picket signs and the media are covering the story. And on and on and on the list goes. Again, the evidence continues to *confirm* her bias that anyone who believes in God (much less Jesus Christ) is nothing short of foolish, if not much, much worse. Never mind that it is the media's *job* to make money through ratings, and good ratings only come through stories with the greatest shock value. No, the obvious conclusion is simply that thinking people would never, ever buy into such God-belief nonsense. After all, if God is like that, why would I, why would *any* thinking person, ever believe in God? (This is a *great* question by the way, which is addressed in *Christian Logic 1*)

Before I go any further, I just want to pause and ask: Can you relate? Does any part of this testimony relate to *your* life experience? Is there a time in your past, where God disappointed you, so you struggled with faith? Is there a time when you read stories about Christians, churches, or pastors in the news and media that caused you to think, "If God is like that, why would I or any thinking person ever believe in God?" Are there times in the past where you have been hurt, perhaps deeply wounded, because you dipped your toe into the pool of faith, only to find the water scalded you? Has a family member or a friend who deeply disappointed you in the past, also caused you to question God or faith in Jesus Christ? If so, then perhaps we are ready to continue. Why? It's because, where God and Jesus Christ are concerned, authentic conversations about Christianity must involve a limp. Put another way, it is *critical* to begin our conversation not with perfect, magically enhanced, fairy-tale, genie-granting-3-magic-wishes ideas of God, rather we begin with the *harsh* realities of life. We begin with our own, messy, dysfunctional lives. We begin with the understanding that God is a *participant* (notice: this is not to say God is the cause of it) in our own, messy, dysfunctional world.

23

To illustrate, I draw our attention to the Christmas story. Well, to the *American* Christmas story. You know the story, but I tell it again. You work all year to be good, for goodness sake. We try not to be bad, because we don't want coals in our stocking. The reason? We all know that Santa Claus is keeping score. Thus, the goal is to be *good enough for goodness sake,* so that on Christmas night, when magic-Santa launches his magic sleigh, he will graciously rest his sleigh and piles of perfect gifts on our rooftop, to magically slide down the chimney, to then leave all the perfect little presents.

On Christmas-Santa morning, we rush down the stairs to find that all our problems are solved. The kids are happy, the dog is happy, we are happy, and the new (and free) Lexus sits in the driveway just waiting for us to drive back to work, to never again experience road rage, spilled coffee on that new dress, or a flat tire. Ahhh, the joy of Christmas. Perhaps we add a quick "thank you prayer" to Santa-Jesus, and then life goes on. This is the god of the American Christmas, if not of America in general. Jesus is Santa Claus, and God's *job* is to put everything under my "tree of life" that I ask-pray for. This includes, God forcing other people to live like I want, love me like I want, and do what I want (regardless of free will), as well as God manipulating *nature* like I want so that my circumstances will become all I need to be happy. Do that, and me and God will get along just fine, thank you very much. I definitely am up for believing in God, if God is like that.

To frame this in other terms, it's almost like we believe God should be a superhero. God has omnipotent, if not magical, powers. The purpose of God's power-magic, is to give good gifts to all of us, especially when we have been good for goodness sake. Or, if not to give good gifts, the purpose of God's power-magic is to fix, solve, correct, and *heal* all of life's wounds whenever life disappoints, draws our blood, or scars us deeply. Thus, Santa-Jesus knows your every thought and deed. Santa-Jesus has the power to manipulate your life circumstances for your good. And because Santa-Jesus loves you, all you have to do is ask, and you will receive. All you have to do is seek, and you will find. All you have to do is knock on the door of Santa-Jesus' home, and He will open the door to give you whatever presents you request. You need more money? Pray to Santa-Jesus. Done! Need a new job? Just pray to Santa-Jesus. Done! You need better heath? No problem, just pray to Santa-Jesus. You need your spouse to quit being a jerk? Presto, Santa-Jesus waves his magic wand and your spouse will no longer do or say those hateful things. Awesome. Well, until Santa-Jesus does *not* give us the gifts we ask for. Then what?

Let's talk about the *real* Jesus for a moment. Hopefully you are familiar with this story too. What a contrast to the American Christmas story. The *real* Christmas story begins with two very poor people, both in difficult situations. Mary is barely a teenager. She has no parents. She has no money. She is a young, vulnerable woman in a society that trashed, abused, oppressed, and openly discriminated against women. Tradition says that Joseph married her more as a favor to the Temple priests than anything else, and Joseph himself had very little to be proud of. Being pregnant with Jesus *before* they were married, Mary and Joseph took the grueling journey to Bethlehem. When they arrived, there was no room at the inn. And let's be honest, if they had had enough money, certainly a room would have been offered. But they didn't, so it's out to the stables they go.

It is important to picture the scene of Jesus' birth. Ever been to an overly used, and not so perfectly kept horse barn? If not, imagine: Manure. Mud. Dirt. Itchy hay. Spiders. Crickets. Bugs. Dirty water. Cold drafts of air coming through the open doors and huge cracks in the walls. Mary and Joseph come here, and immediately Mary begins the final throws of her contractions. Here? Notice, there is *nothing* in this story that reads like a myth or fairy tale. Notice, there is no magic, no presents under a tree, no beautiful wreaths, no warm apple cider on the stove. It is barren, cold, dark, dirty, messy, *real*. The Gospel of John chapter 1 (particularly verses 9-12) sums up the picture well: *and the "world did not recognize"* Him. Why is this, do you think? Why didn't the world recognize Him? Is it not that the world expects God to show up in a very, very different way?

To the movies. Superman. Now *that's* a superhero of mythical proportions for sure. The man of steel. Laser eyeballs. Faster than a speeding bullet. Able to lift mountains. Can fly, even into space. Wow. And how did he enter our world? If you follow the 1978 version of the movie, Superman enters our world in a fireball of a comet, plummeting faster than the speed of sound, literally exploding on the scene as he hit the ground with huge troughs gouged in the earth where he landed. And when grandma and grandpa go to see what happens, there is the god-child, Superman, with his hands raised in the air proclaiming, "Here I am! Come to save the world." Now *that's* the entry of a god, yes?

To Thor: son of Odin, who enters our world only after a tornado extends into the heavens, then there are flashes of lightning and accompanying dust storms as arcs of light and power race across the sky. At the end, Thor falls to the earth with an epic detonation, and he is dressed in scarlet and wielding his mighty hammer, Mjolnir. Awesome. Again, *that's* the entry of a god. Yes, Thor or Kalel, *that's* what we would "recognize" as the savior of the world. In fact, that's what we *want*, because it would make God so easy to spot. Why? Because we want God to act like a god, we want God to meet our expectations of what we want God to be. Contrast that to Jesus, and well, Jesus is just so boring. A baby in a manger and 2 peasant parents? Seriously? How boring is that. I mean really, even Santa has a better story than Jesus. After all, Santa at least has flying reindeer and elves and he gives lots of presents when *he* came. When Jesus came, what did he give us?

To answer that question, we need to turn to one more movie, *Titanic*. If you have seen it, you know the two main characters are Jack Dawson and Rose Bukater. Even if you haven't seen the movie, you know the plot: The Titanic sinks. However, what makes the movie so memorable is the way in which the hero, Jack, emerges. He begins as an arrogant, brash young man who is enamored with Rose. Rose, of course, falls for Jack, and over the course of the cruise, they fall in love. We all know the Titanic is going to sink. What we *don't* know until the end though, is that, as the Titanic sinks into the frigid seas of the North Atlantic, Jack does the unthinkable. He and Rose are facing certain death if either of them falls into the freezing ocean waters. In the end, it becomes clear that only one of them can survive. In his love for Rose, Jack puts her on the floating debris, and he sinks to his death. No fireworks. No arcs of lightning. No hammers. No sleigh and reindeer. Only tears and suffering. No happy endings, only pain. And yet, you would be hard pressed to not call Jack *more* of a hero than Thor or Superman would ever be. Why? Well, that's a pretty good question, isn't it?

Let's talk about Jesus Christ for a moment. Can you imagine, plunging down from the celestial city in heaven into a little baby's body, and your first experiences are screams, dirt, blood, cold, hunger, thirst, and messiness? Naked and cold, strange sights and sounds. Not the expected entry of a "god" to say the least. And lest we forget, Jesus left our world the same way: screams, dirt, blood, cold, hunger, thirst, messiness. Do we also understand that, if indeed Jesus was real, and Jesus was God (which we will discuss later), then Jesus *chose* the path of messiness and dirt, pain and thirst, rather than the path of royalty, Caesar or a Prince of Egypt? Why is this? I personally believe it is precisely because Jesus wanted us to know that he understands *you and your life.* Put another way, Jesus experienced the same life as you and me; life is messy, bloody, often cold and dark, we go terribly hungry and thirsty, and most certainly, real life is *not* a fairy tale, a comic book, or a Santa Clause myth. No, the reality is that life is dark, *very* dark, bloody, and beyond painful at times. So Jesus, a different kind of God, enters our very humble, broken, messy and cold existence, for one single point: to use His life, to put *you and me* on the life raft.

Now, given that, I want us to stop and consider: this is our first piece of evidence, one that the "scholars" rarely talk about. It is Jesus' messy entrance and exit. Jesus never claimed to be nor did He *want* to be perceived as a "god," rather He claimed to be *THE God.* Why? Simple. Jesus *wasn't* like any other god. Compare Jesus to *every other god* you can think of: from the Greek gods of Zeus, Poseidon, Hades, and Aphrodite, to the gods of Hollywood. Thor. Superman. Notice the common thread: They are inhumanly strong. And, they are pretty much immune to true suffering (or at least they don't experience suffering and pain the way "us mortals" experience suffering and pain). But perhaps most importantly, they *all* are considered gods precisely because of their magic superpowers, which they *all* exploit for their own benefit in one way or another, even if they cannot help but being that way. I want to say that again, because it is important: ALL the gods of mythology *exploit their powers for their own benefit in one way or another.* And this, of course, is what mythological gods do, because it is what *makes* them gods. They are all-powerful, and all the world knows it. Take this away, and in truth, they no longer are worthy of a comic book, much less a temple.

Be sure to contrast the stories of the mythological gods from what we know of Jesus Christ. Do you notice that Jesus never exploited His power? Yes, he did a few miracles here and there, but they always were for the purpose *of teaching* and *helping others.* Yes, he healed a few people of blindness or leprosy, or he fed others who were hungry, but it was always with the end of making a mission critical point that He wanted us to *learn about God's caring, loving, and gracious nature.* And never, ever do you find Jesus being inhumanly strong or so invincible that he cannot be hurt. Even in the face of crucifixion, Jesus never exploited his power for himself. And *Jesus suffered, my goodness, did Jesus ever suffer.* With all that power at Jesus' disposal, isn't it a bit odd that Jesus suffered as He did?

Beyond these points, Jesus used His power so *little,* that, in His day, many of his skeptics demanded that Jesus do more to prove or separate himself from us humans. In Matthew 16:1-4, his adversaries demanded, "Give us a *sign, a miracle,*" which of course, Jesus would not be bullied into doing. Which is even *more* ironic is when you consider that many *modern* skeptics say they don't believe in Jesus, *because He did TOO MANY miracles.* Catch that? Many people *today* say Jesus is a myth, because nobody can do miracles, and Jesus did miracles. In Jesus' day, the skeptics said, "You better do more miracles, or we won't believe." What a Catch 22! In *our* day, the skeptics say, "You did *too many miracles,* so I won't believe." In Jesus' day, He didn't do enough. Wow. I want to ask: Which is it going to be? Would you believe in Jesus if he had done *more* miracles or less? Or, is the truth more the fact that, no matter how many miracles Jesus did or did not do, we humans will never be satisfied anyway?

And that indeed is the ultimate question: What will it take for *any* of us to be satisfied where Jesus is concerned? The purpose of this series of *Christian Logic* books, indeed, is to help answer that question. Given that, there are many *assumptions* in this book that I have to make for the sake of time, space and purpose. It is important that, if you have not worked through the initial questions of God and faith, that you do so (to address those assumptions and answer those questions, see the first two books of this series, *Christian Logic* and *Christian Logic 2*). The point of those books is to make the case for a Creator God and answer other foundational questions about faith in general. Given the truths of those books though (that it makes sense to believe a Creator God exists), how would *you* expect this God "to be" for you to believe in and take God seriously? What would God have to do, who would God have to *be,* for you to believe? If God *were* to visit us, how would that need to happen for you to believe in Him?

When you look at Jesus, here are some of the things we see: If you want God to be *real,* living a life that resembles the lives we live too, then Jesus - check. Gracious? Jesus - check. Kind? Jesus - check. Understands our very painful and messy world? Jesus - check. Understands and sympathizes with your hurts and heartaches in life? Jesus - check. Did not use magic wands or take shortcuts for Himself? Jesus - check. Was sacrificial to the point of dying because He loved you and me so much? Jesus - check. I could go on and on. But here is the gist: understanding God simply *cannot* be Santa Clause or a magic genie who grants everybody's wishes, what more are you hoping God will be *than what we already see in Jesus*?

Part of my opening premise is this: Before we even study the evidence, the basic idea of God visiting our world in the person of Jesus (who never considered his power something to be exploited) *sounds nothing like a mythological story.* It doesn't look like a myth, it doesn't quack like a myth, and it doesn't walk like a myth. I want to say that again, because it is critically important. We all know the phrase, "If it looks like a duck, walks like a duck, and quacks like a duck, then it's a duck." The thing is, where myths are concerned, Jesus looks, talks, and quacks nothing like a duck at all, and that's *before* we even consider the historical evidence for Jesus' existence. We don't need a doctoral dissertation in historical criticism to understand what a myth looks like and that Jesus doesn't seem at all like a myth, do we?

Now that being said, we still are going to get into at least a bit of the more complicated historical data. And as we will see, when we use common sense and simply learn the facts, the logical case for the historical Jesus Christ is beyond compelling. In this (as CS Lewis so brilliantly states in his 1972 classic *God in the Dock*), feel free to put *God in the Dock* (an old English term referring to a witness stand), and see where the evidence leads. Feel free to put God in the witness stand and see where the evidence takes you. However, if indeed the evidence points clearly to Jesus Christ being God in our world, then I end with this: The reality is *not* that God is or ever has been under our scrutiny in the dock. Rather, in truth, *we are and have always been in the dock,* and in point of fact, God is wondering what we will do with the evidence we have seen.

Which brings me back full circle to my friend's testimony. At several different points in our conversation, Lizzie made it crystal clear that, for the majority of her young adult life, she fundamentally, absolutely, and unquestionably believed that Jesus Christ was a myth, made up and believed in by people who were weak-minded and incapable of handling the harsh realities of the world, much less life and death. And her rational for this perspective? Unfortunately, 99% of her arguments were based on circular logic, logical fallacy, and confirmation bias. Fortunately for her though, she has now come to the point in her life where she understands, none of that was *logic at all, and she has found transformative healing as a result.* Today, Lizzy will be the first to tell you that one of her biggest mistakes in life was to base her beliefs about God on skewed perspectives on reality and flawed assumptions, all grounded in circular logic and confirmation bias regarding bad experiences and incorrect conclusions drawn from the past. As such, there was a fatal flaw in her arguments before she even began the process of making a case for truth regarding God and what constitutes being a spiritual person. Is this you?

Lizzie's foundational argument? Jesus Christ was a myth. The more I have pondered her perspective, the more I have come to believe that this is the developing majority position of skeptics (in our society at least) to Christianity today. No longer are people concerned with working through the ideas of Jesus being a liar, lunatic, or Lord (we will come back to that later). Why? Because our conversations are *not* beginning with the facts. No longer do we examine the *Evidence that demands a Verdict,* as Josh McDowell likes to say. Instead, we *begin* with conspiracy television shows or books of fiction like *The Da Vinci Code.* We begin with the conclusion that Jesus Christ was a myth or that he had some other life with a wife and children that has almost nothing to do with this historical Jesus. Why? Because we saw it on TV. Why? Because we read it on the internet. Why? Because we had a bad experience regarding God in the past, and our view of spiritual maturity is nothing more than confirming our *alternative facts* than anything else. Then, we use our own sincerity, our own beliefs, our own circular logic and confirmation bias to increasingly confirm if not convince ourselves that what we *already* believe is both right, truth, and, most importantly, *good* for us, even if it is leading us down the road to more and more pain.

So, it is at this point that I want to ask a favor. Consider: If you have chosen the wrong path, every step you take will lead you more and more away from the right destination. As such, let's at least go back to the fork in the road, and in that place, re-examine the true choices at hand. Put another way, my request is this: would you consider at least learning the facts and letting the *real facts* speak for themselves? What you do with the facts? Obviously, that is up to you. But let's learn the basics. The conclusions you draw from the facts, obviously that is your business and yours alone. But drawing conclusions before we even know the facts, or drawing conclusions based off past life experiences or what someone else told you, or how someone else hurt you, or how God disappointed you, will never lead to truth. Isn't one goal of life to actually believe in *the* truth, rather than anything else? If that is you, I want to encourage you: *use your brain,* embrace the questions, seek answers, and treat your investigation into God and Jesus Christ as you would any other rational, logical part of life. If God, if Jesus Christ, does *not* stand up to your investigation, then so be it. You win, because you will know exactly *why* this version of spirituality is not for you. If however your investigation of the facts leads you to discover and perhaps even fall in love with God, then that will be a monumental win, perhaps even of eternal proportions.

CHAPTER 3

History and Facts

"Give me the storm and tempest of thought and action,
rather than the dead calm of ignorance and faith!"
— Robert G. Ingersoll,
The Works Of Robert G. Ingersoll, Vol. iii

L et's begin this chapter with the perspective of Lizzy from her early years: was Lizzie right? Is Jesus Christ a myth? Or, was Jesus Christ a real, living, breathing human being? Can we ever know for sure? Are there facts? Is there reliable evidence? And my answer is, *Yes!* There certainly is more than enough evidence for the very real person of Jesus Christ. And we will discuss it in detail in just a moment. Before we get to that though, it is important to consider the *fact* that *any evidence at all* for the person of Jesus should be considered remarkable, especially given the historical context in which Jesus lived.

Consider the circumstances of life surrounding the person of Jesus Christ. We are talking about *2000 years ago.* They wrote on scrolls of parchment taken from the pithy stems of water plants, with feathers plucked from the local goose, and ink from the local squid shop. And yes, this is a bit of an exaggeration, but in essence they did not have paper, books, ballpoint pins, or laptops to write all this down. Even more importantly, life before the Dark Ages was a life of little to no education, and the economies of the world were largely agrarian. There were no such things as public schools, or community colleges, or Master's degrees for the poor to middle class. People did not generally know how to read at all, much less write. As such, it was very difficult and often incredibly *expensive* to write things down. Why that matters? Ever notice how few stories we have in history of poor people? Compare that to the mountains of information about the powerful and wealthy, about kings and princes. In contrast, Jesus was poor. Mary and Joseph were poor. The disciples were poor. Because of this, having *any* writings about Jesus is remarkable to say the least.

It should also be noted that, 2000 years ago, especially in Bethlehem and the general area where Jesus lived, we are talking about a backwards society, *not* Enlightened, *not* Industrial, much less "civilized" as we understand it. Compared to today's globally connected, IT world, when talking about Jesus' context, we might as well be talking about cavemen with sticks and clubs, scratching their armpits and howling at the moon around a bonfire. It would take 1600 more years before anyone even invented the printing press. I mean seriously, the *Dark Ages* basically started 500 years *after* Jesus died. Before Jesus, we are talking about ancient Babylon, Nebuchadnezzar and the barbarian hoards. It was a world so foreign to us as to be almost beyond our comprehension, which simply must be remembered when filtering expectations for what is reasonable concerning any documentation regarding the life of Jesus Christ. The reason we find ancient Rome *so* amazing, is because they accomplished so many things with *so much ignorance* compared to how "smart" we are today. And make no mistake,

Jesus grew up far, far from Rome, in a backwards town with backwoods parents.

Beyond all that, it simply cannot be overstated the importance of the status of Jesus and his parents in their society. Jesus was born to poor parents who never did or had anything in life. Jesus grew up in a small town of bread bakers and farmers. He never wrote a book. He never led an army. Jesus never held a political office. He never had any money. He often used a rock for a pillow. He never went to college. He never scored a touchdown. He never did *anything* we would associate with greatness. So tell me, why would *anyone* write anything about Him? Why should *any* evidence exist *at all* for the person of Jesus Christ? The "truth" is, anyone who expects *more* evidence than we already have about the person, life and teachings of Jesus is grossly and deliberately ignoring the realities of Jesus' life and times, how the recording of history works, the agrarian and uneducated world in which Jesus lived, and the lack of resources and abilities Jesus or his disciples would have had to record any information at all. In fact, it is remarkable to say the least that we have what we do have, much less that we have *so much* information about Jesus as we do.

Because of this, we should *expect* most of the evidence we have about Jesus to be circumstantial. In this, skeptics argue that Jesus is necessarily a myth because most of the evidence we have is circumstantial. By circumstantial, I am basically saying that the information does not come from Jesus himself or professional historians. Rather, we know most of what we know of Jesus from all that happened *after* Jesus lived, such as the growth of the early church, the revolution in Jewish culture, the lives of the disciples, or the writings of the disciples. And since there are so many great books already in print regarding the biblical writings of the disciples (ie, how the Bible provides evidence for the historicity of Jesus), I have no intention of going into those details here. It should be stated that there is a *mountain* of evidence in the biblical texts that at some point needs to be part of this conversation. Even so, I limit our time to just a few, bigger picture points for your consideration.

First, no "professional" historian would have covered Jesus in the "media." Why? As outlined above, it is because Jesus was not rich and famous, he was not a ruler, he had no power, no army, no nothing. Why would a historian waste their valuable time and money on a nobody? Remember, historians had to make a living. Put another way, just like our media and news outlets today, the motivator for most media (historians) is *to get a paycheck or to become famous,* preferably both. No paycheck? Then no book. If it doesn't get ratings from the people paying the bills, over time, the news will not report it, no matter how important the story may be to the public. One of the biggest criticisms of the news media today is that they are neglecting the important stories for the sensational, no matter how irrelevant the sensational stories may be. It was the same in Jesus' day. In this, there was absolutely *nothing* they could have written about Jesus Christ that would have helped pay the mortgage. The Romans simply could care less about this penniless preacher from Nazareth.

Second, as the old illustration goes, if you are standing in a building, and 45 people come inside with umbrellas open and they are soaking wet, is it any *less likely* that it is raining outside, even though you never experienced the rain firsthand? Make no mistake, for those who want to dismiss the circumstantial evidence of the disciples, the growth of the early church by tens of thousands of people, the remembrance of Jesus' death in communion, or any of the other evidence about Christ that comes *after the fact* clearly points to lake full of rain. The skeptics who dismiss circumstantial evidence as irrelevant to the case for the historical Jesus Christ are intentionally ignoring the most common sense, logical evidence of all. Just like *any* piece of evidence admitted to a court case, the key is to simply consider the source, realize the potential biases inherent to the source, and use *all* the information, evidence, testimonies, etc to come to a conclusion when it is time to reach a verdict.

One more preliminary note concerning evidence from the Bible. Read about Jesus for yourself in the biblical accounts of Matthew, Mark, Luke and John and let them speak for themselves. Give it the eye test. Give those writings the smell test. The old cliché is a good one, "If it looks like a duck, walks like a duck, and quacks like a duck, well, it's probably a duck." Regarding the question of Jesus being a myth or not, do the biblical stories about Jesus sound mythical? Do the teachings of Jesus sound like the teachings of Zeus, Poseidon, or any other mythical god? Or do the life and teachings of Jesus sound like a real person to you? In reality, if a skeptic has to resort to complicated and far-reaching theories to explain away the "common sense" evidence both in the Bible and outside of the Bible that suggests Jesus was a real person, well, doesn't that tell us all we need to know? Typically, the simplest answer is the correct answer. Typically, the most logical answer is the right one. Setting aside complicated hypotheses and dissertation-motivated conspiracy theories, do the books of Matthew, Mark, Luke or John *sound* like lies, hoaxes, or fiction to you? Do the books of Matthew, Mark, Luke or John sound like any fiction you have ever read? The easy, obvious answer is *no*. As such, of course they are not fiction.

One more piece on the "smell test" of the Gospels. As you read the accounts of the disciples regarding these teachings of Jesus in the Gospels, it is critical to note that they are all *different, even to the point of having discrepancies!* And that is a *good* thing. Scholars call this the synoptic "problem," but I would like to suggest that this is not a problem at all. Instead, it is a *solution.* Solution to what? It is one of the solutions to the skeptical view that Jesus was a myth, because the Gospel discrepancies actually provide evidence that the Gospels are *not* fabrications. Mark does not give the exact, same version of Jesus' teachings as Matthew, and neither does Matthew and Mark tell it the same as Luke. Luke, Matthew and Mark tell it differently than John. Matthew and Luke tell the temptation accounts in *different orders.* John talks about the Last Supper in ways that almost seem to contradict the other writers. This matters because these variances in their stories about Jesus are a *key* piece of evidence as to their validity. Why? Because if it was all a fabricated hoax by the disciples, they most certainly would have conspired to *get the story straight and tell it the same way.*

Imagine two scenarios in a court case for a moment. In scenario A, 45 witnesses who were in a bank are called to provide testimony regarding "what they saw" in a murder investigation. As each witness is called to the dock, they give *exactly* the same testimony. They use the same words. They use the same language. The suspect was seen entering the bank, he went up to the teller and pulled a gun, he demanded money, the security officer intervened, then the suspect shot the security officer and ran. Witness after witness, there is no variation at all in the story they tell, as to what they saw and how the murder happened. Hold that thought, but shift to scenario B.

In scenario B, 45 witnesses from a murder case are also called to the witness stand. This time though, every witness tells a *different version* of the story. One sees the suspect enter the bank, but instead of go to the teller, he was standing in line like everyone else. Then, when the person in front of him (an off-duty security guard) reached the teller, he *began* to draw a gun, at which time the suspect grabbed the gun and intentionally shot the man in front of him. Another witness testifies that the gunman didn't intentionally shoot the man in front of him, rather, they were fighting for control of the gun, when the gun went off. Another witness saw the off-duty security guard actually demand money from the teller as he was drawing the gun, and the suspect was being proactive to take the gun away from the security officer. Another witness says he saw several other men with guns at the back of the bank. Another witness says there weren't other men with guns in the back, however there were members of the *mob* standing in the back of the bank. And on and on the witnesses go, every story is different, yet every story is both believable and closely related to the testimony of the others. To this point: when it all comes out of the wash, who are you going to believe? The 45 people who told *the exact same story?* Or, are you going to believe the 45 people who all tell the story differently, yet threads of everything they all say begin to assemble a very different puzzle and picture indeed?

My point here is that no one would believe the 45 people telling the same story. Why? Because no two people *ever* see and interpret the data of life in exactly the same way. If ever that *does* happen, you can be assured that the witnesses have fabricated, colluded and conspired to cover something else up. In other words, the more exactly the same the story, the more likely the lie. Where it concerns the biblical evidence for Jesus in the Gospels, the discrepancies between Matthew, Mark, Luke and John are indeed quite pronounced. However, the obvious explanation of this point is that they were simply writing *from memory what they saw and heard.* When it all came out of the wash, their memories led to discrepancies, because none of them saw, perceived, or understood Jesus, or the evidence for Jesus, in exactly the same way. In the end though, when you piece together the evidence from *all* the witnesses, the story is compelling indeed. Which finally brings me to the evidence itself, beginning with the non-Christian witnesses, then we'll circle back to a few final thoughts as to what the disciples themselves had to say.

The evidence for Jesus Christ is generally divided into three categories: 1. Christian History; 2. Jewish History; 3. Greco-Roman History. Beginning with the Greco-Roman world, it is absolutely critical to remember that we should *not* expect to hear *anything* about Jesus Christ from the perspective of Rome. Again, Jesus was not rich, he never wrote a book, he never led an army, he never did anything normally associated with greatness. Instead, Jesus was a penniless preacher from Nazareth, raised by poor parents, in a backwoods part of the world that the Romans would have considered about as important as swatting a gnat away from buzzing your drink. And yet. And yet. Tacitus. Famous Tacitus. Rich Tacitus. The *professional historian* Tacitus, Roman senator, orator, ethnographer, and probably the most revered and trusted of all Roman historians, Tacitus actually wrote about the person of Jesus Christ. Did he write much? Of course not. Why would he? And yet, what we have is a priceless treasure for those looking for evidence to debunk anyone claiming Jesus was a myth.

The story is a bit complicated, and for details, I refer you to your local library. For our purposes, a quick summary should suffice. There was a fire in Rome in the early 60s AD, and a general conspiracy arose against Emperor Nero, that he intentionally set the fire so he could build what he wanted. Think of it as an extraordinary "it's demo day" plan. Looking for a scapegoat for the cause of the fire, Nero (who hated Christians) attempted to blame Christians for the catastrophe. To be very clear, no one has *ever* said that "Christians from the time of Jesus are a myth." That is important, because the historicity of *Christians* immediately after the time of Jesus is indisputable fact, which no one has ever called to question. There simply is *far* too much evidence for even the most antagonistic skeptic to pull that one off. The annals of Rome have far, far too many accounts of Christians to deny their historicity. As such, the *only* question is whether historical Christians *from the time immediately after the supposed death of Christ*, who claimed to follow Jesus Christ, fabricated and lied about everything we know of Jesus Christ. That point is *very* important. So, be sure to pause a moment and absorb that last statement before moving on.

Back to the story: Tacitus enters our equation, because the *professional historian* Tacitus was recording the events for the annals of Roman history regarding Nero's renovation project. To summarize, Tacitus writes that these Christians (who Nero said caused the fire) were followers of Christ, who had been executed by Pontius Pilate in the reign of Emperor Tiberius. All of these facts by the way, are consistent with what is recorded in the New Testament. The *twist,* for anyone reading between the lines though, is that it is highly unlikely that Tacitus would have remotely *cared* to help the Christian movement by validating Jesus' presence in the world. Tacitus was no friend to the Christian movement, and he most certainly had no interest in Jesus Christ personally. As such, it is beyond important to our conversation that Tacitus does not even *hint* that Jesus Christ was a hoax or a fraud, or that these early Christians were followers of a mythological figure. Not once do we find any mention of Jesus' story being nothing more than the invention of desperate and pathetic disciples who were willing to be executed for a man they all knew never existed. Instead, what we have from Tacitus is exactly *what we would expect,* which is simply stating the fact that Jesus Christ was the man put to death by Pontius Pilate under the Emperor Tiberius. Study Tacitus for yourself for the details.

Let's move on to another historian, this time the Jewish historian, Josephus. Josephus was a Jewish priest. Most certainly, Josephus was *not* a Christian either. As we would expect, Josephus was also wealthy, growing up in an aristocratic family in Palestine and then moving to Rome. Early on, Josephus had several Roman Emperors who supported his work as a historian, but the tides turned when he decided to join the Jewish revolt against Rome in the mid-60s AD. In a very interesting turn of events, Josephus wound up being the historian for the Emperor Vespasian, from which he would continue his life in relative wealth and fame, even though some of that fame would be because many Jews saw him as a traitor. Not to be deterred, Josephus would continue to write and record history for many years. To this day, Josephus is considered one of the most reliable historians from early Rome. And while this is an oversimplification, Josephus makes reference to Jesus Christ, who was called the Messiah, as well as a few others we find in the biblical account (especially James, the brother of Jesus). Study Josephus for yourself for the details.

Regarding other historical sources, it should be mentioned that at least half a dozen or so other, less reliable writers-historians mention at least something about Jesus. Because they are unnecessary to our conversation, I leave it to you to explore, research and study them if that interests you. But more important to our purpose, the final piece of conclusive evidence I offer here is that, not one single account exists, from *any* historian from the Greco-Roman-Jewish world, that claims Jesus Christ did *not* exist. And while that may sound a bit unimportant, it should not be underestimated how powerful an argument it *would have been* if the Romans or the Jews *who were there* would have said "Jesus never existed, or "it never happened." If Tacitus had said that Jesus was a hoax, it would have held incredible weight. If Josephus had said anything remotely like Jesus was a lie of the disciples, skeptics today would be all over that document like flies to "you know what."

And remember, *antagonists* were there all along the way. It was antagonists who crucified Jesus. It was antagonists who scattered the disciples. It was antagonists who would *later crucify* the remaining disciples. Make no mistake, if Jesus Christ was a myth, and if Christianity was a rising political and religious force that threatened the Jewish establishment, those very Rabbis and other Jewish leaders would have made it crystal clear to the world that Jesus never existed in the first place, much less that his crucifixion never happened. <u>And yet not *one single document, not one single paragraph, not one single statement* from all of Greco-</u>

Roman-Jewish antiquity says anything remotely like that. Curious to say the least, if you are looking for evidence *against* this historical Jesus.

Which brings us to the Christian witnesses, beginning with the *place* of Israel. And let's just use common sense, logic for a moment. If the accounts of Jesus Christ in Matthew, Mark, Luke and John were fictitious, then wouldn't it make sense for at least *some* of the *places* described in the biblical account to be fictitious as well? Where did Jesus teach and preach? Around Galilee. On the Mount of Olives. At the Temple. And you can visit those places today. Where was Jesus born? Bethlehem. Go see it for yourself. The place where they "claim" Jesus was crucified? Golgotha. You can take a tour. The garden of Gethsemane where Jesus was betrayed. Check. The Jordan River where Jesus was baptized. Check. In fact, *show me* any "place" in the biblical-historical account of Jesus Christ *that does exist.* And you can't. Why is that do you think?

To the disciples. Again, let's appeal to common sense, simple logic. Except for Judas (hung himself) and James (tortured by being boiled in oil), tradition (and thus history) says that every last disciple wound up being executed, because they would not stop teaching other people about the very real life of Jesus Christ. Peter? Executed by crucifixion. Andrew? Scourged and crucified, preaching about Jesus until he died. James? Executed by Roman sword. Philip? Crucified. Bartholomew? Crucified. Thomas? Killed with a spear. Matthew? Killed by sword. The "other" James? Stoned to death. Thaddaeus? Crucified. Simon the Zealot? Crucified. And all for what? For a man they all knew was a hoax that *they themselves* made up? Seriously? What logic, what sense does it make for them all to be horribly, painfully murdered, in so many different places, in so many different *parts of the world,* if they all knew Jesus was a lie, a hoax, a myth? Maybe you want to argue that the disciples were myths too? Oh yeah, then Joseph and

Mary must have been myths. And Pontius Pilate was probably a myth too. And Mary, Martha, and Lazarus were all myths? I would submit that it takes far *more faith* to believe all these people, and all their stories were myths, than it does to simply accept what history tells us. Jesus lived, that's for certain, and all these disciples were willing to be tortured and executed talking about the very real life of Jesus Christ.

And there is much more. So much more. Tradition tells us that Mary, Jesus' mother, would go on to become a leader of the church in Ephesus. Curious if she knew "her son" Jesus was a fabricated hoax. Or was Mary a myth too? The church itself was formed by hundreds, then thousands, then tens of thousands of people, many of whom *were there* when Jesus lived. Who in their right mind would think, of all those thousands of people, no one ever stood up to "tell the truth" about the hoax of Jesus not being a real person? Or consider all the accounts of Jesus, the historical reliability of the New Testament manuscripts, or the biblical evidence itself. Literally thousands of books have been written, *fields of study created* (like *Biblical Archeology,* the study of *ancient biblical languages,* the study of *ancient biblical manuscripts, etc etc)*, and so much more exists that point to the validity and credibility of the historical Jesus. But again, that is not for us here, but it is to say: Given the preponderance of information from antiquity still available today regarding Jesus Christ, it is beyond compelling to see that no credible shred of evidence has ever emerged that *denies* Jesus Christ being a real person.

Which leads me to what I believe is the most compelling evidence of all. How about the teachings themselves of Jesus Christ? Back to Dr. Phil. The ultimate question is simply this: Do these teachings from Jesus Christ *actually work?* The most damning evidence of all would be if, when a person actually *followed* the teachings of Jesus, the end result is brokenness, hurt, conflict, suffering or pain. And while even a cursory study of

Christian history must admit that the teachings of Jesus most certainly *have* been used by messed up, abusive, power-hungry, narcissistic people in ways that cause and result in suffering, I would argue that Jesus Himself, never, ever in a million years, would have supported people like that, regardless if they quoted His teachings or not. It has already been said that Jesus didn't exploit his power *for his own* personal interests, so it stands to reason Jesus would not support *other people* exploiting Him and His teachings for *their* purposes. For anyone to think that He would allow or even support them in doing so is beyond preposterous. In truth, it is a clear indication that these folks never truly understood what Jesus was teaching in the first place, choosing instead a very different path more indicative of the broken human condition than anything Jesus had to offer.

No, for those willing to see it, the real issue is *not* what other hypocritical Christians, pseudo-Christians, or people abusing Jesus' teachings for their own selfish motives have done with what Jesus taught, rather the question *is:* when we take Jesus Christ and his teachings on their own merit, do His teachings "work?" And my answer is categorically, "Yes!" Why? Because, when you love and forgive and show mercy as Jesus teaches, when we are the Good Samaritan like Jesus teaches, when we "do unto others" as Jesus teaches, when we follow Him as suffering servants to lift up and love and care for the hurting and broken world around us, again like Jesus teaches, the bottom line is that these things really do work. They actually *do* lead to peace like Jesus promises.

These writings from *Jesus* are transformative, life-changing, and life-*giving.* From Jesus' teachings on how to find forgiveness, to his teachings on how to rid your heart of anxiety, to his teachings on how to have better relationships in life, to so much more, they simply work. If the Dr. Phil question is engaged, "How's that working for you?" The answer to Dr. Phil is, "Well, when I actually follow what Jesus himself says*, it does work*; it *is* working." There is no more powerful testimony than life experience. If it is true, it should work in everyday life, and this is where Jesus simply corners the market. There is no teacher in human history who has had more of a profound impact on the human race than Jesus Christ. There is a reason that people who follow the teachings of Jesus have better lives and wind up being better human beings: it's because Jesus spoke *truth*, and when you do what He says, your life is healed and transformed.

Is there more? Of course. We could go into the motives for the disciples to lie about Jesus. What would be their motive? Why would they *die* teaching about this Jesus, when, if they simply claimed to author the teachings themselves, they probably could have finished their life in comfort and peace? No, the most logical answer is that, indeed, Jesus existed, and Jesus did and said the things recorded in the scriptures. We could go into all the reasons people reject Tacitus and claim his historical accounts are as unreliable and mythological as Jesus himself. We could discuss why people say Josephus' accounts are the made-up lies of later frauds, who wanted to use Josephus' name to add credibility to their ideas. And so, so many other conspiracy theories and fanciful hypotheses trying to subvert the obvious truth. But you know, at some point, you just have to back away and say, *enough*. It doesn't matter where you are in life, there will always be antagonists, as there will always be friends. Someone always is "out there" who disagrees with what rational, logical people say, as there will also be those who agree. To that end, the key is to calm all the voices, and *let the evidence speak for itself*. Then, after personal study and reflection, draw conclusions based on what you have learned, *not what other people say*.

Thus the appeal: What about you? Given the witnesses you have heard, what does the testimony suggest to you concerning Jesus being a real, historical person or not? Use your brain. Draw your own conclusions. If you do, my hunch is that you already know where the evidence leads. However, let's not make up our minds quite yet. Onward to a study of the cross.

CHAPTER 4

Evidence for the Crucifixion

"The heart of Christianity is a myth which is also a fact.
The old myth of the Dying God, without ceasing to be a myth
comes down from the heaven of legend and imagination to the
earth of history."
— *C.S. Lewis, God in the Dock:*
Essays on Theology and Ethics

After hearing from Tacitus, Josephus, the disciples, and teachings of Jesus himself, it isn't too much of a stretch to conclude that Jesus Christ was not a myth. Even so, there are parts of Jesus' life, especially his crucifixion and resurrection, that demand investigation as well. The reason? Because plenty of people are willing to concede that Jesus was a historical figure, but those very same people often are *not* willing to admit that Jesus was either crucified or resurrected. For some, like those who believe in conspiracy theories from fictional publications like *The Da Vinci Code,* they dismiss the crucifixion, arguing that Jesus chose a different path, including being wed to Mary Magdalene, having children, and basically living happily ever after. For others, they believe Jesus was indeed crucified, but they reject the resurrection, arguing that such "miracles" are nonsense. Pretty much every possible ending of Jesus' life and story is promoted by someone, which yet again demands that we consider the evidence to reach our own conclusions.

To address these questions and continue in our investigation, I want to discuss both the reasons why the resurrection and the crucifixion are historical events, as well as *why* they are important to the meaning of Jesus' life and message as well. I take this dual approach to address a growing trend, which is, people tend to pick and choose the parts of Jesus they like, and they dismiss whatever it is they dislike or don't understand. Put another way, it is not enough to simply explain the evidence for the crucifixion. That part is relatively easy, and if that was all there was to it, few would doubt its historicity. However, when you couple the *meaning* of the crucifixion with the *historicity* of the crucifixion, well, that's where many of our problems emerge. But you cannot have one without the other. Put another way, I am trying to avoid the illogical approach to this topic by many people who say, "I don't believe the crucifixion happened, because I don't believe in its *meaning."* Either it happened or it didn't. And if it happened, it either means what it means, or it does not. There are no alternative truths regarding the crucifixion or the resurrection either. There is truth and fact, then there is everything else. Our goal is to discern truth and fact, and to avoid everything else. As such, for the rest of our study, we engage a bit of both history and theology.

Beginning with the meaning of the crucifixion. Why does it even matter that Jesus was crucified? After all, isn't it enough to say Jesus lived, taught, and *somehow* died, but the cause of death is not really relevant? The point being, isn't it the *teachings* of Jesus that matter, not his death? Why should anyone actually care if Jesus was actually crucified or not? And to answer that question, we have to travel all the way back thousands of years to the Jewish sacrificial system described in the Old Testament.

The story begins with the context surrounding Genesis 22, especially the developing view of justice that would later be cemented in the *Code of Hammurabi.* This view said that, if you hurt me, I get to hurt you in equal (or worse) measure. The idea being, an eye for an eye, and a tooth for a tooth. If someone hurts you (sins) or you hurt someone else, a price must be paid; always, a price must be paid by the transgressing party. In many places of the world today, this is still the norm. I would suggest, in *most* people's minds, the *Code of Hammurabi* is the de facto standard of justice from which most of us operate. You hurt me? Justice will only be served when you are hurt in equal or worse measure.

The *problem* with the *Code of Hammurabi* though, is that, for 99 out of 100 people, we only like the *Code of Hammurabi* when it applies to *other* people. In other words, we fundamentally believe in and embrace the idea of justice that other people should *get hurt* in proportion to how much they hurt me. However, no one likes the idea that *I* should be hurt in proportion to how much *I* hurt other people. In other words, we want forgiveness without consequences, but we want *them* to feel the full force of consequences and retribution, often to the extreme. I might add one other problem with the *Code of Hammurabi,* which is: more often than not, in practice, the *Code of Hammurabi* does not lead to justice, rather it leads to war. Why? Because all it takes is for *one* person to forget or refuse to admit "who started it," and you then have endless fighting with endless retribution, the results of which is nothing less than a vicious cycle of eye-taking and tooth-breaking. Just look to the ongoing conflict between Israel and Palestine for an example. Harmony, true justice, and peace are rarely found in retribution unless you simply annihilate your enemy. Probably not the best possible outcome. But that's for another story.

To our story in Genesis 22. With Abraham, God is beginning to introduce to the world a new system of justice, a system that is very, very different from the *Code of Hammurabi.* Where the *Code of Hammurabi* is based on retribution, the system embraced by Abraham is a covenant code based on grace, forgiveness and sacrifice. It's the idea that, if you truly repent, you can actually be forgiven of your sins *without* retribution. Now that being said, it is *not* the idea that you can be forgiven without a price being paid or consequences faced. But it is at least possible in this new covenant code of Abraham to not *personally* pay for what you have done. Instead, in the beginning at least, Abraham, and those like him, would lay hands on an innocent animal, transfer your guilt to the animal, then sacrifice it as payment for your sins. And usually, the sacrifice of this unblemished animal would be sufficient. I say "usually," because when it came to this particular day for Abraham in Genesis 22, the rules changed a bit.

To bring us up to speed with our story in Genesis 22, the short version is that Abraham and Sarah had wanted children for some time. They both were old though, and any hope of having children had been long forgotten. To their surprise, God informs Sarah that she will have a son, which happens, and they call him Isaac. As previously mentioned, they both had adopted this covenant theology embodied in the sacrificial system. It was the idea that, to experience true forgiveness, an animal, usually a lamb, would be sacrificed for atonement. Atonement basically means, becoming "at one" with God. In this context, some point down the road, God commands Abraham to go to a local mountain, Mount Moriah, to make his usual sacrifice. By the way, Mount Moriah would later become the same historical place where King Solomon would build the Temple. Again, very real history, no myths here.

Again, you can visit the place today. Anyway, the twist in our story is that, rather than an unblemished lamb, God tells Abraham to take his only son, Isaac, and use *Isaac* as the sacrificial offering. Preposterous. Even more preposterous, Abraham *agrees,* and off he goes, with Isaac, to the sacrificial altar.

Isaac's perspective on this? Business as usual, except the lamb was missing. In Genesis 22, Isaac would ask Abraham, "Dad, where is the lamb for the sacrifice?" Abraham replies, "God will provide the lamb for the sacrifice." And it continued to be business as usual until they reached the altar on Mount Moriah. At that point, Abraham binds up Isaac and engages the transference of guilt ritual. Then, to the horror of Isaac, Abraham actually pulls the knife to finish the job. Again, preposterous. Horrible. Who would do such a thing? In a relief plot twist though, at the last minute, God tells Abraham to stop, to release Isaac, and then God provides a ram for the sacrifice. We are intended to ask: what in the *world* is going on here? Why would God put Abraham and Isaac through all of that? Make no mistake, God wanted us humans to learn something very important from that story.

Fast forward to Moses and the Exodus story. Long story short, the idea is that the Egyptians had enslaved the people of Israel, who were descendants of Abraham and Isaac. Through a series of events, Moses had become the leader of the Israelites (also called Hebrews), and Moses' mission was to be God's instrument to free the Hebrews from the oppression of slavery under Egypt and Pharaoh, so they could journey to and enter the Promised Land. Moses demanded to Pharaoh, "Let the Hebrew people go." Pharaoh refused, followed by 9 plagues, culminating with the 10th plague, the *Death Angel,* which is where, for our purposes, things get interesting.

At this point, rather than provide a summary, we can read it for ourselves from Exodus 11 (*CommonEnglishBible.com*): "¹Then the Lord said to Moses, "I will send just one more disaster on Pharaoh and the land of Egypt. After that, Pharaoh will let you go. In fact, he will be so anxious to get rid of you that he will practically force you to leave the country. ⁴ "This is what the Lord says: About midnight I will pass through Egypt. ⁵ All the firstborn sons will die in every family in Egypt, from the oldest son of Pharaoh, who sits on the throne, to the oldest son of his lowliest slave."

Then in Ex 12, "²¹ Then Moses called for the leaders of Israel and said, "Tell each of your families to slaughter the lamb they have set apart for the Passover; ²³ For the Lord will pass through the land and strike down the Egyptians. But when he sees the blood of the Lamb on the top and sides of the doorframe, the Lord will pass over your home. He will not permit the Death Angel to enter your home.

The point here is to see that the blood of the lamb literally meant salvation for the people of Israel, Abraham's people. The blood of the lamb literally provided the *key* to them being delivered from the oppression of Egypt. The blood of the lamb was the final ingredient to the people of God being able to go to the Promised Land. The blood of the lamb meant the *Death Angel* would pass over their home, allowing not only for their freedom, but also for them to be free *together*. And this was so incredibly important to the Jewish people that, literally thousands of years later, they are still celebrating the *Passover Remembrance* to this day. And at every *Passover* feast, a lamb shank bone is used as a memorial to the original Passover Lamb from so many years ago, that saved the lives of their firstborn and created the events that led Pharaoh to change his mind and allow the Hebrews the freedom to leave.

Fast forward 1500 years to the time of Jesus Christ. In John 1:29, Jesus has grown up and he is ready to engage his public ministry. Before this begins though, Jesus comes to John the Baptist, to be baptized in the Jordan River, as so many others had been doing before him. The twist here? John the Baptist looks at

Jesus and says the most curious thing, "Behold, *here comes Jesus, the Lamb of God*, sacrificed for the sins of the world." Several times later in Jesus' teachings and ministry, Jesus himself would state that his mission was to be sacrificed as part of God's redemptive plan for a broken world (see Matthew 16-17, 20; Luke 9; Mark 8-9; John 12 and 20). The idea is that, where it is preposterous for us to even *consider* that God would ask Abraham to sacrifice his only son, Isaac, here with Jesus, it *is* God being willing to sacrifice his only son, Jesus, to pay the ultimate price for the sins of the world. Jesus *was* the one, true, and final sacrificial Lamb of the covenant code. In other words, like Abraham, Isaac, and every other person who has ever lived, what we *deserve* is justice according to the *Code of Hammurabi.* However, what God offers is a new way, a new truth, a new path to life that offers forgiveness, redemption and freedom from guilt for any and all who accept the blood of the lamb, the sacrifice of Jesus Christ, the lamb of God, who died for the sins of the world. Which finally brings us to the crux of the crucifixion.

Hebrews 9:11-14 (*CEB.com*) "Christ appeared as the high priest of the good things that have happened. He passed through the greater and more perfect meeting tent, which isn't made by human hands (that is, it's not a part of this world). [12] He entered the holy of holies once for all by his own blood, not by the blood of goats or calves, securing our deliverance for all time. [13] If the blood of goats and bulls and the sprinkled ashes of cows made spiritually contaminated people holy and clean, [14] how much more will the blood of Jesus wash our consciences clean from dead works in order to serve the living God? He offered himself to God through the eternal Spirit as a sacrifice without any flaw "

1 Peter 1:18-20 (*CEB.com*), "[18] For you know that God paid a ransom to save you from the life you inherited from your ancestors. And the ransom he paid was not mere gold or silver. [19] He paid for you with the precious lifeblood of Christ, the sinless,

spotless Lamb of God. [20]God chose him for this purpose long before the world began, but now in these final days, he was sent to the earth for all to see. And he did this for you."

Why does the crucifixion matter? Because without the crucifixion, God doesn't care, and He did *not* do anything all that radical or important for you or me. Without the crucifixion, there is no sacrificial Lamb of God. Without the crucifixion, there is no covenant code. Without the crucifixion, there is no answer to the problem of sin for the human race. Without the crucifixion, the only alternative is "eye for an eye and tooth for a tooth," which means the only alternative is incessant violence and paying each other "back" in equal or worse measure. Without the crucifixion, John 3:16 is a lie, and God has not given His one and only Son that whoever believes in Him might have life. Instead it is the same as every other story: God is not, has not been, and will not truly be involved in the human story of pain and suffering. Without the crucifixion, God doesn't really understand, and in truth, God doesn't care. In essence, without the crucifixion, *the entire ministry and life and teachings of Jesus Christ become hollow and worthless.* Which leads, I believe, to the ultimate reason people attempt to reject the historicity of the crucifixion.

When it comes to arguments against the crucifixion of Jesus Christ being a historical event, you have to look long and hard to find *anything* that makes even a semblance of sense. Part of the reason is because of the difficulty in refuting the historical record we have already discussed from Tacitus, Josephus, and the circumstantial evidence too. But part of the reason is because, if you believe Jesus *lived,* then you also have to explain how he died. And account after account consistently tells the exact same story, the story most of us have already heard and that is the most common sense reading, that Jesus died on a cross at the hands of the Roman executioners.

Alternatives to this story? There are several, but most are so unreliable as to be worthless for study, such as *The Da Vinci Code* fiction that implies Jesus married Mary Magdalene, had kids and lived happily ever after. Nonsense, and by the way, *fiction*. But two perspectives do stand out compared to the other theories. The first theory basically says, at some point before the actual crucifixion, Jesus escaped, and another person fooled everyone by taking Jesus' place and going to the cross as Jesus' substitute. The arguments *against* anything like that happening are simply mountainous compared to any evidence we have that a substitution event occurred. In fact, what we know is that the Romans, the Jews, and the crowds were watching like hawks from the arrest of Jesus in Gethsemane all the way to Golgotha. We know that Jesus was betrayed by one of his disciples, a disciple who certainly would have known if it was *not* Jesus. We know the Pharisees had been plotting to execute Jesus for years, and they knew him well. And so many other antagonists were involved too. As such, there is just no possible way an imposter could have taken Jesus' place and fooled anyone, much less everyone.

The only other even remotely viable theory that Jesus was not killed by crucifixion is that indeed, Jesus was crucified, but He did not actually die. The idea is that, even though everyone (including the trained Roman soldiers who did this for a living) thought Jesus had died on the cross, in the end, Jesus was still hanging on with a breath of life. Once they put him in the tomb (the cave), the cool fresh air revived him, and Jesus went on to roll the stone away and go live the rest of His life in relative peace. The reason this argument is dull indeed is because of what Jesus had been through. The flogging had ripped most, if not all, of the skin off his back, which in and of itself would be enough to kill most people. Add to that, this theory does not deny that Jesus in fact *was crucified.* Even a cursory study of Roman crucifixion would see that death is the inevitable result. Even more, after the entire ordeal, the soldiers pierced Jesus' side to be certain he was dead. The point is simply this: rip the skin completely off a man's back, nail him to a cross, then stick a spear in his side, and he dies. This is a medical fact. No human body could possibly endure what Jesus went through and live, much less, get up a few hours later, push a mammoth boulder out of the way without the guards (who were posted outside) noticing, and then go on to be embraced by the disciples with but a few scars to show for it. It simply makes no sense.

Do your own research, but I would suggest that there are no other theories worth even considering concerning the crucifixion being a myth or a fake. As such, that leaves us with only one, final option. It is the common-sense option. It is the *logical* option. And, yes, it is the *Christian* option. Yet again, we have looked at the evidence, and it yields *Christian Logic.* Study the evidence, and if you believe Jesus lived, then you also must accept that he was executed via crucifixion. If you accept that Jesus was executed via crucifixion, then you also must accept that Jesus *knew* this was going to happen. If you accept that Jesus knew this was going to happen, you also must accept the entire "Lamb of God" concept for the atonement of human sin. And if you accept that, well, this means that God actually cares about you and me, that grace is God's alternative to the *Code of Hammurabi,* and God provides a route to freedom from the guilt and oppression caused by our sin. And if you accept *that,* well, it just changes everything about both who God is and who we are, how both God and us humans deal with our mistakes and transgressions in life, as well as why we exist, and where we are headed in the life to come. A fact punctuated by the final chapter in our story, the historicity and meaning of Jesus' resurrection.

CHAPTER 5

Evidence for the Resurrection

"The worst type of person is the one who
is sincerely believes they are right,
but they are sincerely wrong, and they have no clue." – me

Our investigation is drawing to a close, but a few more pieces of evidence are still worth considering before we wrap up this particular study. As a quick recap, we now have considered Tacitus, Josephus, the disciples, a few teachings of Jesus himself, the crucifixion of Jesus, and a few alternative theories regarding all of it. The only other question remaining for our purposes regarding the historical Jesus is the question of the resurrection. And why should we study this one? Because plenty of people are willing to concede that Jesus was a historical figure, and even that Jesus was crucified, but many of those very same people often are *not* willing to admit that Jesus was resurrected. After all, it makes some sense that Jesus was a historical figure. It also makes some sense to think Jesus was crucified. However, what sense does it make to think that *anyone* could be resurrected from death? Surely *this* piece of Jesus' story is myth. Isn't it? Or, is it?

To address these questions and continue our investigation, I want to discuss two parts of the resurrection: 1. The reasons why a thinking person would believe the resurrection is a historical event; and, 2. *Why* the resurrection is important to the meaning of Jesus' life and message in the first place. The irony here is that the meaning behind the resurrection is a far more difficult piece to comprehend than the event itself. Put another way, it is natural to assume that the historicity of the resurrection is the impregnable challenge of logic to overcome. However, I would argue that the more profound piece of this equation is *why* the resurrection of Jesus Christ is so profound, and thus critical for all of us to understand. As such, it is only when you couple the *meaning* of the resurrection with the *historicity* of the resurrection, that the transformative power of the resurrection of Jesus Christ becomes evident. And I might add: just as in every other part of life, so also with this topic, there are no alternative truths regarding the resurrection of Jesus. There is truth and fact, then there is everything else. Our goal is to discern truth and fact, while laying aside everything else.

So, why does it even matter that Jesus was resurrected? After all, isn't it enough to say Jesus lived and taught amazing things? Isn't it enough to say Jesus was one of the greatest teachers the world has ever known? Isn't it enough to say that Jesus was a really good guy? Why should anyone actually *need* to care if Jesus was actually resurrected or not? Even more, no one is raised from the dead. There is no empirical proof. None of us has a shred of evidence. As such, no logical, thinking person would *ever* believe there is life after death, would they? The science is clear: human beings return to the dust, and that is where they remain. Forgotten over time. Gone forever. And certainly, no one *comes back* from death to visit us in this life. That's ridiculous, and it simply never happens. No, instead we know death, and all we will ever know is death. Come on, get real. Resurrection simply doesn't happen. Or does it? As for an answer, it all depends on who you listen to.

In 1 Cor 15:1-14 (*CEB.com*), Paul sums it up like this: "15 Brothers and sisters, I want to call your attention to the good news that I preached to you, which you also received and in which you stand. ² You are being saved through it if you hold on to the message I preached to you, unless somehow you believed it for nothing. ³ I passed on to you as most important what I also received: Christ died for our sins in line with the scriptures, ⁴ he was buried, and he rose on the third day in line with the scriptures. ⁵ He appeared to Cephas, then to the Twelve, ⁶ and then he appeared to more than five hundred brothers and sisters at once—most of them are still alive to this day, though some have died. ⁷ Then he appeared to James, then to all the apostles, ⁸ and last of all he appeared to me, as if I were born at the wrong time. ⁹ I'm the least important of the apostles. I don't deserve to be called an apostle, because I harassed God's church. ¹⁰ I am what I am by God's grace, and God's grace hasn't been for nothing. In fact, I have worked harder than all the others—that is, it wasn't me but the grace of God that is with me. ¹¹ So then, whether you heard the message from me or them, this is what we preach and this is what you have believed.

¹² So if the message that is preached says that Christ has been raised from the dead, then how can some of you say, "There's no resurrection of the dead"? ¹³ If there's no resurrection of the dead, then Christ hasn't been raised either. ¹⁴ If Christ hasn't been raised, then our preaching is useless and your faith is useless. ¹⁵ We are found to be false witnesses about God, because we testified

against God that he raised Christ, when he didn't raise him if it's the case that the dead aren't raised. [16] If the dead aren't raised, then Christ hasn't been raised either. [17] If Christ hasn't been raised, then your faith is worthless; you are still in your sins, [18] and what's more, those who have died in Christ are gone forever. [19] If we have a hope in Christ only in this life, then we deserve to be pitied more than anyone else."

At least one major point to notice from Paul here: when he says, "some of you say, 'There's no resurrection of the dead'" (vs 12b), the clear premise of that statement is precisely that people were saying, "There is no resurrection of the dead." Even more to the point, antagonists in Paul's day were saying, "There's no resurrection of the dead" *in the context* of Paul discussing the resurrection of Jesus Christ *from the dead.* Why this matters is because these statements by Paul in 1 Corinthians 15 are clear appeals for these very antagonists to go talk to the eyewitnesses that Paul has just named - Cephas, the Twelve, the 500, James, and Paul too. How is this relevant to our case? Because Paul wrote these words in the mid-50s AD.

In the mid 50s AD, these eyewitnesses of Jesus' resurrection named by Paul *were still alive.* It cannot be overstated how important this historical context is to the reliability of the facts recorded in the scriptures. Here in 1 Corinthians, Paul is naming a *modern* issue of people not believing the resurrection events. But in contrast to us today, those people could literally go interview the eyewitnesses. And it is no stretch to think that whoever had questions, was skeptical or truly interested in answers would have interviewed many of the 100s of eyewitnesses named by Paul. Historically, the church flourished immediately after the 50s AD, which *logically* points to validity of the testimony of all those people. If indeed Paul was lying about so many witnesses, or if the witnesses were lying, the logical result would be the death of the early Christian movement, or in the least, a preponderance of materials also being written saying that these people were frauds or crazy. Instead, all history tells us is that the church grew exponentially, with the primary *reason* behind such exponential church growth being the resurrection of Jesus itself. Hard to justify the historical growth of the church immediately after Jesus' death, if all those people knew it was based on deliberate lies or nut-job, crazy people.

To a related question: Why was (and is) the resurrection of Jesus such a fundamental part of the exponential growth of Christianity in the world? Why not simply believe the moral teachings of Jesus that work with our modern worldview, but throw out everything else? Why is Paul so adamant (1 Cor 15:3) that, if we throw out the resurrection of Jesus Christ, then *all* of Jesus' teachings are worthless? Why would Paul scoff at the idea of a person accepting Jesus as a great moral teacher, even though they reject his resurrection from the dead? And there are many answers to those questions, some theological, some moral, some historical. I stick with the historical answer: It is because, without the resurrection, we would not have *any* teachings of Jesus to even consider today. Why? Common sense says that if Jesus had died and remained in the grave, then we would have never heard about Him or His teachings at all. And that is a big statement, so be sure to stop a moment and process it. But I say it again, *without Jesus' resurrection from death, there would be no stories of Jesus for us to consider, because Jesus would not have made enough impact on human history for anyone to record his life or teachings in the first place.*

As a recap, we remember that it was Jesus' *trial and crucifixion* that got the Romans' attention, not his teachings. It was Jesus standing before Pilate. It was Jesus taking his cross to Golgotha. It was Jesus being nailed to the cross by the Romans. And, *it was Jesus' followers* who said Jesus was crucified, dead, and buried, but on the third day He arose from the dead. Never do you hear of Tacitus or Josephus quoting the *teachings* of Jesus. They didn't care. At that point in time, *history* didn't care. Instead, what mattered was what actually happened around Jesus trial and crucifixion, *and the events immediately thereafter.* To be very clear, if Jesus had died and remained in the grave, *nothing would have happened, much less been recorded thereafter.* If Jesus had only been a great teacher, and not been crucified and raised from the dead, the followers of Jesus would have dispersed, and that would have been the end of it. Even if Jesus had been a great teacher, but then simply been executed by the Romans, then history itself would have forgotten Him forever. The only differentiator is the resurrection. Why?

Back to the story of Jesus himself. Clear and simple: Jesus was a nobody, an absolute nobody. He came from nobody parents. He made nobody friends. And, in historical terms, Jesus left this world a nobody as well. The theological ramifications of Jesus, who was God incarnate, *choosing* to be a nobody are nearly unfathomable, but that is not for today. What *is* for today are the historical facts of his situation. Jesus was born to a peasant woman. Mary and Joseph were so poor that they couldn't send ahead for a hospital, hotel, doctor or even wet-nurse. The first 30 years of Jesus' life are so insignificant that we know almost nothing, except that Jesus liked to go to the Temple without telling his parents (and get in a lot of trouble). He did not go to high school or college. He did not get a masters or doctorate degree. He didn't write a book. He didn't hold a public office. He didn't command an army. To the point: Jesus didn't do *anything* in those early years worthy of anyone remembering, much less historically recording what happened in his life.

When Jesus was 30 years old, he began his public ministry by gathering a few uneducated, nobody disciples. And he did "disciple" them with some fairly impressive teachings, however Jesus also taught some really *weird* stuff too. Jesus said He and

God were one and the same. Jesus said He was the same God that spoke to Moses at the burning bush. Anyone who thinks Jesus was just a great ethics teacher needs to hit the pause button and remember that Jesus said He was God. Seriously? That is crazy talk! And he made these points so incredibly clear that the Jewish leaders attempted to execute Him several times for blaspheme. In three years, they *would execute* Jesus for only 1 reason - Jesus said He was God.

Over the course of those 3 years, we should expect Jesus to change the world and do incredible things, right? But what did Jesus actually *do?* Think about it: Jesus Christ has had *more influence on the history of the world* than any other figure in all of human history. No other person in the history of the human race has had a more profound impact on the course of world events. So, certainly Jesus would have eventually commanded an army and conquered the known world? Nope. Surely, Jesus would have invented things that changed the world, like revolutionizing industry, or a printing press, or *something?* Nothing. What about great scientific theories? Nope. What about amassing wealth and using his money to change the world? Nope, Jesus was penniless. Well, could he at least shoot a basketball like LeBron James? Nope, basketball was not invented yet. Listen: Jesus never did *anything* we associate with greatness during His life. Let me say that again, as it is just too important to miss: Jesus never did *anything* we associate with greatness during His life, so why would He ever become the most influential human being in world history? He usually slept on the ground. Jesus owned nothing more than the clothes on His back. Jesus had so little money that He depended on the people around Him to take care of Him.

So, what made Jesus so special *in this life?* The highlight reel of Jesus' life, the most famous thing that happened to Him, is that He claimed to be God, so the Jews crucified Him. And lest we think there is anything special about being crucified by the

Romans, they had been crucifying people for a 100 years before Jesus and would continue crucifying people for a 100 years after Jesus. Even crucifixion itself wasn't that big of a deal back then. And to make Jesus' story even *less* interesting, his few disciples *fled in disarray* at His crucifixion. Tell me, where in that story is *anything* worth remembering? Put another way, is this the biography of someone you would expect to be the greatest, most influential person in all of human existence? Of course not.

And yet, it is incontrovertible, no one else in the history of humanity, has even come *close* to influencing our world as much as Jesus. Others would love to claim the top spot, but they just don't have the numbers. Over the course of 2000 years, there have literally been billions upon billions of people who claim to be Jesus followers, both from his time all the way up to present day. These are people whose lives have been *transformed* by becoming a disciple of Jesus themselves. Several billion more people respect his teachings, and billions more at least think he was a decent guy. All from a penniless teacher of Nazareth who barely traveled 100 miles past his city of birth, and He did nothing remarkable during His life, a life that ended, as did many others at the time, on a cross. Given all of this, what is the LOGIC to explain how Jesus has had such a significant influence on planet earth and human history? And the answer always, always comes back to the resurrection. *Without the resurrection, there is absolutely no reason why anyone would ever remember Jesus again.* But with the resurrection, quite literally, history changes radically.

The complicated series of events that led to the resurrection are too extensive for our purposes here. But a quick summary is: Jesus had told all his disciples what would happen, *before* it happened. Jesus had explained that, as one with the Father who was the Son of Man and Son of God (Old Testament terms for God), Jesus was also the Lamb of God, whose blood must be spilled, and He himself must be slain, for the forgiveness of the sins of the world. Jesus would also say, as the Son of God and Son of Man, He was the great "I AM" that existed before Abraham was born, at which time, the Jews picked up stones to kill him. But all of these were titles, designations the religious authorities new stood for God himself, that Jesus also knew the disciples would later piece together as they began to discover what it all meant. On various occasions, Jesus told them He would die, that His mission was to go to Jerusalem, that His purpose was to become bread and wine, so his blood would be shed for the sins of the world. But not simply for forgiveness in this life, the entire *point* was forgiveness so that anyone who would believe that God might give His one and only Son would then inherit eternal life in God's home forever. Which is where it *really* gets interesting.

The closer Jesus got to the cross, the *more* He began to teach the disciples about eternal life. Do you think that was a coincidence? At one point, Jesus came right out and said He *was* the resurrection. Wow. At other times, He would teach the disciples about God having residences in heaven for all who believe. At other points, Jesus would teach them about having a soul, and preparing that soul for the life to come *after* this life. Jesus would allow some of the disciples to see other "dead people" in a post-death state at His transfiguration. And sure, we can pick and choose and throw out the various stories that don't align with our science today. Yet even still, the mountain of teachings from Jesus concerning heaven and the afterlife is impressive. In fact, it is not a stretch to say, if you remove all of Jesus' teachings that in some way, shape or form relate to heaven and the afterlife, then you are left with very few teachings at all. Which again points to the logical conclusion: without the resurrection to *back up* all Jesus had been teaching on heaven and the afterlife, Jesus would have been long forgotten as a well-meaning moralist, but who also had very warped ideas of self-worth and identity when it came to believing Himself to be God.

But that's not how events unfolded. Instead, well, let's read it straight from one of the sources. John 19 (*CEB.com*), "²⁸ After this, knowing that everything was already completed, in order to fulfill the scripture, Jesus said, "I am thirsty." ²⁹ A jar full of sour wine was nearby, so the soldiers soaked a sponge in it, placed it on a hyssop branch, and held it up to his lips. ³⁰ When he had received the sour wine, Jesus said, "It is completed." Bowing his head, he gave up his life. ³¹ It was the Preparation Day and the Jewish leaders didn't want the bodies to remain on the cross on the Sabbath, especially since that Sabbath was an important day. So they asked Pilate to have the legs of those crucified broken and the bodies taken down. ³² Therefore, the soldiers came and broke the legs of the two men who were crucified with Jesus. ³³ When they came to Jesus, they saw that he was already dead so they didn't break his legs. ³⁴ However, one of the soldiers pierced his side with a spear, and immediately blood and water came out. ³⁵ The one who saw this has testified, and his testimony is true. He knows that he speaks the truth, and he has testified so that you also can believe. ³⁶ These things happened to fulfill the scripture, *They won't break any of his bones.* ³⁷ And another scripture says, *They will look at him whom they have pierced.*

³⁸ After this Joseph of Arimathea asked Pilate if he could take away the body of Jesus. Joseph was a disciple of Jesus, but a secret one because he feared the Jewish authorities. Pilate gave him permission, so he came and took the body away. ³⁹ Nicodemus, the one who at first had come to Jesus at night, was there too. He brought a mixture of myrrh and aloe, nearly seventy-five pounds in all. ⁴⁰ Following Jewish burial customs, they took Jesus' body and wrapped it, with the spices, in linen cloths. ⁴¹ There was a garden in the place where Jesus was crucified, and in the garden was a new tomb in which no one had ever been laid. ⁴² Because it was the Jewish Preparation Day and the tomb was nearby, they laid Jesus in it."

Then, just like everyone who had come before Him, and like everyone who would come after Him, Jesus was dead. *Hopefully* he was in God's hands now, but how could anyone know for sure? Well, that's the thing, and that is indeed the *true* difference between the story of Jesus Christ, and the story of every other human being who has ever existed. And make no mistake, this is *precisely why Jesus stands out from all other human beings in all of human history.* Why? Because Jesus' death was not the end of His personal work in the events of human history. For after the crucifixion, 3 days after to be precise, when the women went to the tomb, it was empty. Then, the resurrected Jesus met some of them outside of the tomb. The resurrected Jesus would also meet the disciples in the Upper Room. The resurrected Jesus would meet other disciples on the road to Emmaus. The resurrected Jesus would later appear beside the Sea of Galilee. As already mentioned, the resurrected Jesus would later appear to over 500 people. Even skeptics like Saul of Tarsus were converted by the resurrected Jesus. And to be very, very clear, countless numbers of people have experienced the resurrected Jesus *since* that time too. We can discount them for various reasons, but it doesn't diminish the *fact that their stories exist too.* Stories from people like Charlie Winslager, who, just a few years ago, told me personally that he literally saw the resurrected Jesus receive his wife, Leila Jo, when she was on her deathbed and breathed her last breath. This is the true difference between Jesus and everyone else. Regardless if you believe them or not, there are more stories than a person can count regarding experiencing the resurrected Jesus *even today.* Who else in history can say that?

So what are the theories *against* the resurrection of Jesus? And remembering that we have already examined the evidence for Jesus being a historical person and dying by crucifixion, one of the final questions for our purposes is, "what happened to Jesus' body?" It simply went missing. How? Put another way, *since we have already proven* that Jesus was a real, historical person, one of the most important questions we must answer regarding the resurrection is: What happened to Jesus' body after He was crucified? In our previous chapter, we already addressed the illogical arguments that perhaps Jesus didn't die during the crucifixion, then He rolled the stone and walked away. Yeah right. We also looked at the theory that someone took Jesus' place, so that it wasn't actually Jesus who was tried before Pilate and crucified. Which makes no sense. So what theories are left to us as to what happened to Jesus' body? To which, our alternative options can generally be divided into 3 categories, from weakest to strongest: 1. Forgotten Tomb; 2. Theft; 3. Hallucination.

First, you could argue that everyone simply forgot which tomb Jesus' body was buried in. In essence, they lost the body. And while this is possible, it is just *so* improbable. Why? Because Jesus' mother, Mary, was there the entire time. Because the Roman guards were there the entire time, even posted outside of Jesus' tomb. Because Jesus was an "enemy" of the Jewish state, and the entire reason they crucified Jesus was because He claimed to be God, and everyone was well aware of Jesus' teachings about eternal life and resurrection. There is no *possible* way the Jewish authorities who went to so much trouble to kill Jesus, would simply walk away without a bit of follow-up after his death, which is precisely why guards were placed at the tomb. To "forget" where they placed the body, or somehow position their guards at the wrong tomb, is absurd. And then this: the process for burial in those times was very clear: You prepare a body for burial, then you bury them with a burial service. Even though they did not have modern funeral homes as we do, the process was still similar, with the body being taken for "preparation" and then, on the appropriate day, a funeral and subsequent "permanent" burial would proceed, with appropriate words being said, prayers prayed, etc. There was never a true funeral for Jesus, neither was there a burial, *because the body was missing.* And you simply have to explain this somehow. When the ladies arrived to make final burial preparations, the body was gone. As previously mentioned, to say that they lost the body or forgot where the body had been placed is just nonsensical. Which leaves us with the idea that they *had* Jesus' body, but he was still dead. In this theory, if the disciples had stolen Jesus' dead corpse, and then used it to proclaim Jesus was raised from the dead, how would that work? Put strings on Jesus' dead corpse arms, put his dead corpse behind a veil in the dark, wave His dead corpse arms in the air with the strings, and then try to imitate Jesus' voice? You get the image of some psychopath carrying Jesus' crucified body around like a Pinocchio puppet, talking through cracked lips and pulling Jesus' arms up and down while proclaiming that Jesus is alive. Seriously? The point here is to emphasize the absurd extremes skeptics must go to, to come up with any reasonable explanation against the resurrection.

Second, to explain this missing body, some have argued that the body of Jesus was stolen. And for my 2 cents, this is at least a bit more plausible than losing the body or carrying the corpse around, but saying Jesus was alive. To the theft argument, we could work through why neither the Romans, nor the Jewish authorities, nor the disciples of Jesus himself would have allowed the body to be stolen. Too much was at stake for all parties involved. The Roman guards would have faced severe discipline, perhaps even death, if they had allowed the body of Jesus to be stolen out from under their guard. The Jewish leadership *knew* that Jesus had made claims of resurrection, so there was no *way* they would let the body out of their sight. And the disciples of Jesus, including His mother Mary, were deeply grieving and had every intention of giving Jesus a proper burial. Even if one or two or several of the disciples formulated this grand scheme to steal Jesus' body and claim His resurrection, Jesus' mother Mary most assuredly would have never allowed it, and the Romans and Jewish authorities would have gone to extreme precautions to keep the body safe. If anyone stole Jesus' body, make no mistake, they would have had *no allies* from either the Romans, the Jews, the family of Jesus, or, we can guess, from most if not all of the disciples themselves. Beyond that, back to the previous arguments for resurrection, simply stealing Jesus' body does nothing to answer the question of a resurrected Jesus appearing to so many people after His death.

Speaking of Jesus appearing to so many people, the one argument remaining that *does* at least make a little sense, is the argument of hallucination. That being, Jesus was crucified, dead and buried, but then, rather than *actually* appear to all those people, they simply all had *hallucinations* of Jesus appearing. This is how you might explain away my friend, Charlie Winslager's "interpretation" of what actually happened when his wife died. Why? Because Charlie saw Jesus, *but only Charlie* saw Jesus. But the story of the disciples is fundamentally different from my friend Charlie. Why? In the case of Jesus' resurrection, all those people saw *the same, or at least very similar* hallucinations. How is this relevant? Well, again, back to using our brains, back to common sense, back to logic. If you and 12 other people are in a room, and you all see a "ghost" at exactly the same time, is that a hallucination? Even more, let's say that "ghost" talked to you all, and you all heard the exact same thing? Hopefully you get the point. The *nature* of hallucination by default means that no 2 people could ever see it or experience it at the same time or in the same way. If 2 or 3 people are gathered together, and they experience the *same phenomenon,* then that same phenomenon is very real indeed. 100s of people saw the resurrected Jesus, many of them together at the same time. This simply cannot be explained away as a hallucination.

Which leaves us where? Hard to believe, but do the math, work through the logic for yourself and you will see, there is no other viable argument remaining out there in all the world for the historical reliability of Jesus' life, death, *and resurrection.* It all actually happened. Before you go any further, think carefully about that statement, for it is a gamechanger. It all actually happened. There is no other viable argument remaining out there in all the world for the historical reliability of Jesus' life, death, *and resurrection* than this: It all actually happened.

As to other arguments for the resurrection, they are numerous. And other authors and scholars far more competent than me like Josh McDowell, Lee Strobel, CS Lewis, Adam Hamilton, and so many others have written volume upon volumes of books on why it makes complete sense to believe in the resurrection of Jesus Christ. Arguments such as: 1. It makes no sense for all the disciples to be brutally executed for proclaiming a resurrected Jesus they all knew they were lying about; 2. Jesus' mother, Mary, would go on to become a leader of the church in Ephesus, a church proclaiming the resurrection of her son that she knew was dead and buried; 3. Very early in the formation of the church, they would celebrate Communion in remembrance of Jesus' sacrifice and Easter in remembrance of His resurrection, which makes no sense if the body of Jesus could still be found or if no one had a shred of proof of Jesus being resurrected; 4. Also early in the formation of the church, Christians would practice the sacrament of baptism, which explicitly linked death and burial (going under the water) with new life and resurrection (coming out of the water), again, which makes no sense if the body of Jesus could still be found, or if there was no proof at all of His resurrection; and so much more. The issue is not really if there are any arguments for the resurrection of Jesus Christ. Clearly, the evidence is compelling. And it is compelling for *logical, thinking people.* But not only is the evidence compelling for the resurrection of Jesus. We have one more issue to discuss before wrapping up this conversation, and that is this: the evidence is compelling for *everything being true* that Jesus lived, taught, and promised. And for that, we turn to our final chapter of this study.

CHAPTER 6

The Final Verdict:
The Truth Will Set
you Free

"The truth about an animal is far more exciting and altogether
more beautiful than all the myths woven about it."
— Konrad Lorenz, Lads Before the Wind:
Diary of a Dolphin Trainer

If your child were to do something really stupid, and then
you were to ask them, "Why did you to that?" Would it
bring great pride and joy, would it lift your spirits, to have
them respond, "I don't know. Just because." I don't know. Just
because. Obviously, it's a cop out. But the truth of the matter is that
we often *don't* have specific reasons for doing or believing many of
the things we do and believe in life. Instead, we just believe it, and
that's the end of it. And even if it is a lie (alternative truth), if we

believe it, we sincerely think it must be true. And if we sincerely think it is true, then we also thin it must be good for us. The unfortunate result is that sincere thinking based on alternative truth (lies) are NOT good for us, because wrong thinking eventually leads to poor choices and a life filled with regret and guilt, not to freedom. Wrong thinking, no matter how sincerely right you think you are, invariably leads people to make poor choices that lead to regret, mistakes, wrong turns, and a laundry list of unintended, undesirable consequences. Rather than knee-jerk reactions to the world around us, how much better off would we *all* be if our daily behaviors were driven by sound logic, critical thinking, well thought out plans, and proactive, strategic decisions that are grounded in truth and wisdom?

Jesus makes an interesting, if not ironic, statement in John 8:32. "The truth will set you free." I find this ironic because, when someone actually adheres to the "truth" when responding to the world's challenges, such truth invariably winds up restricting our freedoms. For example, there is a "true," best practices, way to be physically healthy. You *avoid* bad foods and eat healthy foods. You exercise *properly,* as improper exercise can cause injury. You get adequate sleep, which never happens without disciplined scheduling. Many truths to both learn and remember regarding being physically healthy. Yet notice, *the more truth you live by, the more restrictive your diet and daily physical routine must become.* If you "live free," by eating anything you want and not disciplining your body through regular exercise, you will eventually become overweight, sickly, prone to heart disease, and worse. The point is this: You may be *free* to eat anything, live anyway, and ignore healthy habits, but such free behavior will eventually imprison you in doctor visits, medications, clogged arteries, and increasing physical pain and suffering. Freedom is not liberating. Freedom is not what sets us free. Instead, it is *the truth* that sets us free, if we freely choose to live into the truths we know.

How many people in our world believe that "freedom" is liberating, while "rules based on truth" are oppressive? How many people feel that freedom is the answer to most of life's problems, and the great oppressors in life are those people or things that don't allow me to do what I want and when I want it? In contrast, how few people believe that the great oppressors in life are the areas in our own thinking that are not based on wisdom and truth, areas where our own thinking is flawed, faulty, and defective? What if the real oppressors in life are our distorted conceptions of truth, such as where we have not learned that peace, love, hope, and joy are internal choices? Or, that experiencing peace, hope, or joy are 100% dependent on how you *think* about yourself and the world around you, rather than manipulating the world to your satisfaction? When will we learn that, where spirituality and God are concerned, the great issue is not in changing your life into right circumstances, but in having a right perspective regarding those circumstances?

So here's the thing: true freedom has nothing to do with getting to do whatever you want, whenever you want. True freedom has nothing to do with being able to think anything you like, regardless if you are right or wrong. That is our "fatal flaw" in defining freedom. No, true freedom is found when you live into the truth, such that you are emotionally, physically, and spiritually healthy enough to enjoy the life you have been given, even with all the flaws life throws your way. In this, freedom is simply the *choice* that comes *as* you follow the truth or not. Even before that, freedom is the *choice* to learn the truth itself, *so that you can know what the best choices for yourself might be.* Why? Because a lack of wisdom and sincerely believing "alternative truth" leads to poor choices, and poor choices ultimately lead to *prison.* Get that? It doesn't matter how sincere you may be, if you break the Law (the rules, the "truth"), you get fined, go to prison, or worse. The Judge will never say, "Well, they were drinking and driving with a blood alcohol level of 2.3, but they sincerely believed they were OK. So, no big deal, give them their keys back." Not gonna happen. No, the *truth* and only living *within the truth* will not only set you free, but it will also *keep* you free. Anything else, and it is prison time.

It is beyond ironic that so many people in our society view the truths of God in terms of limiting our freedoms. The idea is that a spiritual life is also a limited life of prison and self-imposed rules and regulations. It is also the idea that God is somehow on God's heavenly throne barking down orders and commandments, rules and laws to us peon humans, because God is bored. Or, God likes to use His big stick to poke the ant bed of humanity, because God enjoys stirring up trouble by telling us what to do and getting us to fight over it. Is this really how it works though? Put another way, is there *any* area of life where being ignorant of truth or defiantly ignoring truth actually leads to life and life in abundance? Is there *any* area of life where, if playing in the street leads to kids getting hit by cars, that both knowing the truth and following it isn't actually a *good* thing for all involved, especially the kids?

Where God is concerned, it cannot be overstated how applicable this idea of truth and freedom is for us to experience health and abundance in life. Why? Because only truth liberates. Only truth heals. Only truth leads to transformation. And I am not talking about whatever truth you and I already sincerely believe because of confirmation bias. Nor am I talking about alternative truth that isn't truth at all. Instead, I am talking about whatever truth that is "out there" that is *actually* God's truth for all time, that transcends our frail human understanding, and that inevitably is the ground upon which all existence stands. Which leads me to the ultimate question about Jesus Christ, and the pinnacle issue and purpose behind this particular book.

Jesus Christ claimed to be *the Truth.* Jesus claimed to not only understand, but actually to *embody* the Truth- God Himself, the Incarnate Word, the Alpha and Omega, the Beginning and the

End, the Answer, the Solution, the Prime Mover, the great "I Am," of it all. *Huge claims!* So huge in fact, that the leaders of Jesus' day who actually understood what Jesus was saying were absolutely infuriated and terrified by it. They would ask Jesus specifically, "Who do you think you are, making such claims like this?" And Jesus would respond, "I and the Father are one and the same" Or, "Before Abraham was, I am." Or, "I am Bread of Life." "I am Living Water." "I am Light of the World." *In other words, I am God! That's who I am!* And the more Jesus continued to press his point, the angrier his adversaries became, to the point that they literally crucified Him for it.

The *reason* for the crucifixion. This really brings us to the heart of the matter at hand. Lots of people in our world like to talk about Jesus as this "really nice guy." Or, Jesus was a great teacher. And they wear crosses around their necks. They even put a cross tattoo on their bulging biceps. But when pressed with the question, "Who do you say that Jesus is?" The answers rarely produce anything of substance. Instead, we often regress back to elementary school with answers such as, "Jesus was a really nice guy!" Or, "Jesus was a great moral teacher." Or even, "I don't really know, but I like the idea of a cross; it's just cool." I just have to ask: Is that it? Is the cross nothing more to us today than a cool tattoo?

And thus, it is to the cross that we pull this together, for on that very cross, the very same cross that adorns so many necks and is tattooed forever on so many body parts, we are confronted with the once and for all question: ***Why was Jesus crucified?*** I ask it again, Why was Jesus crucified? This is a HUGE question, because it ultimately gets to the fundamental truth claims of a man who literally claimed to *be* Truth. This is a HUGE question, because, if you believe "freedom is found in the discovery of and adherence to truth," then the cross signifies the Truth *himself* who came into our world to show us, teach us, and help us find freedom through the truths He taught and lived. Why was Jesus crucified? One reason, and one reason only: Jesus claimed to be *God*, the one and only Truth, who came into our world to show us the way to a better life, both now and into eternity. This is the *only* reason Jesus was crucified. Miss that, and you miss everything.

Now, part of the reason people "miss" that point is that we just have a hard time believing in God in general, much less that God would visit our world in the form of a human being. And part of the reason for *that* is because, in our ever-expanding global world, we are continuously being exposed to more and more competing "alternative truths" as to God or variations of "being a spiritual person" in the first place. From atheism, to agnosticism, to all the world religions, to every cult and sect and offshoot religious voice in-between, we have a smorgasbord of alternative truths today. The phenomenon is similar to people from 3rd world countries who experience an American grocery store for the first time. There are too many choices. They are overwhelmed. And often, they wind up hating the entire experience, even though what they always wanted is right there on the shelves for the taking.

So let's simplify this entire "God equation" just a bit. Do you realize, in the scope of all human existence, you basically have only 4 choices about God? You can choose atheism, which means there is no God. Easy enough. Of course, the implications of believing "there is no God," are far from easy, but that's not for this study. Second, you can choose Agnosticism, which means, there might be a God, might not, but we can never know, so why bother? Third, you can choose *any of all the world religions except Christianity*, which are ALL works-based religions. Yep, you heard me right, I am saying that every single world religion, cult, sect, and offshoot religious group can be lumped into one, single category. Why? Every last one of them says the same thing: The right path is to *do what they say*. Think carefully on that one, and you will see the logic of it.

Then we come to the only alternative. Then we realize what makes Jesus Christ so special, unique, and the world-changer He was. This is where we *finally* come to understand why this penniless preacher from Nazareth, who never wrote a book, never led an army, and never did "anything else we associate with greatness" was actually so great. Here it is: Jesus said, "I am God." And as God, let me tell you what God is like, so you can stop guessing. Fundamentally, God is love. But not love as you humans define it. No, God is love as *God* defines it, that being, God loves all of you, forever and for all time, God has, does, and will always love you all. God says His type of love is unconditional. It is underserved. God's love for you is unmerited. You cannot earn it, nor can you stop it, thwart it, or lose it. As a perfect Father or Mother loves their children unconditionally, so also God loves you. Sure, God is disappointed when we mess up or make poor choices, but that never, ever changes God's love for you. Sure, God teaches us "rules" and wants us to obey them, but not to earn His love, rather it is simply to help us make better choices and thus have better lives of abundance, while avoiding negative consequences of bad decisions. But underneath it all, there is only 1 Truth about God, 1 Way to understand God, 1 Narrow Gate to be in God's presence, and it is the Path of freely choosing to accept God's love and love God in return. There is no other truth, no other way, no other gate, no other path. Jesus was very, very clear on this. And so they crucified Him for it.

Again, why did they crucify Jesus? Always, always, we must come back to the "why" of the cross. And Jesus absolutely left zero room for debate on this. On this point at least, Jesus left no grey areas, no middle ground between Himself and the options of the world. No, Jesus said, "I am the Way, I am the Truth, I am the Life, and no one comes to God, unless they come through Me." Period. Sounds exclusive, I know. But it's the most inclusive statement God could ever make, because Jesus is saying, No one comes into the presence of God, unless they come through the door of love and grace, "through Me." For there is no other way, except the way of God's unconditional love for you and me. And Jesus says, I am God, here to tell you Myself, that this is how "I am."

Towards the end of Jesus' story, the trial regarding Jesus' fate concludes like this: Mt 26 (*CEB.com*) "⁶² Then the high priest stood up and said to Jesus, "Well, aren't you going to answer these charges? What do you have to say for yourself?" ⁶³ But Jesus remained silent. Then the high priest said to him, "I demand in the name of the living God that you tell us whether you are the Messiah, the Son of God." ⁶⁴ Jesus replied, "Yes, it is as you say. And in the future you will see me, the Son of Man, sitting at God's right hand in the place of power and coming back on the clouds of heaven." ⁶⁵ Then the high priest tore his clothing to show his horror, shouting, "Blasphemy! Why do we need other witnesses? You have all heard his blasphemy. ⁶⁶ What is your verdict?" "Guilty!" the Sanhedrin shouted. "He must die!"

And they literally killed Jesus immediately thereafter. Again, why did they crucify Jesus? It was because of His "blasphemous" public teachings. CS Lewis in His book *Mere Christianity* puts it like this: "I am trying here to prevent anyone saying the really foolish thing that people often say about Jesus, that "I'm ready to accept Jesus as a great moral teacher, but I don't accept His claim to be God." That is the one thing we must not say. For a man who was merely a man and said the sort of things that Jesus said (about being God) would not be a great moral teacher. He would either be a lunatic- on the level with the man who says he is a poached egg- or else he would be a lying devil of Hell. You must make your choice. Either this man was and is the Son of God; or else a mad man or something worse. In fact, you can shut him up for a fool, you can spit on Him and kill Him as a liar. Or, you can fall at His feet and call Him Lord. But let us not come up with any patronizing nonsense about His being a great human teacher. He

has not left that open to us. He never intended to." (Lewis, CS.
(1952) *Mere Christianity: The Shocking Alternative.* New York,
Simon and Schuster Publishing, p. 56.)

Profoundly and timelessly insightful, the logic of CS
Lewis is incontrovertible. And be sure to think back on how this all
ties back to where we started. There are no alternative facts here.
There are no competing truths. There are no logical fallacies. The
end result of all of this conversation is for Jesus to leave us with a
simple choice about who He was and what He was about. There is
the truth of the situation, then there is everything else that is not
true. There is the correctness of the situation, then there is
everything else that is incorrect. *If you do not believe Jesus was a*
myth, then you must then conclude that Jesus was crucified. *If you*
believe that Jesus was crucified, then you also must have a reason
why Jesus was crucified. *Since Jesus was crucified for claiming to*
be God, then that finally leaves us with only 3 choices. All of this
work, all of this study, all of this time, and it boils down to 3 simple
choices: First, Jesus was a nutcase. He truly believed He was God,
but He wasn't. If so, Jesus might as well be a poached egg. Second,
Jesus was a liar. He said He was God, but Jesus knew full-well He
wasn't. If so, we also should chunk all Christian teachings, because
they are based off the insidious lies of a very, very adept deceiver.
Or, or. Notice, if you rule out the "myth" choice, which we have
already addressed, and you also rule out the lunatic or liar choices,
then notice, Christian Logic leaves us with *only 1 final choice:*
Jesus was God, and Jesus indeed was the Way, the Truth, and the
Life.

And, it is this Truth that will set us free. Set you (and me)
free from what? Well, that is not for this study. But it is worth
saying that Jesus' entire life, ministry, teachings, death and
resurrection were all about setting us free from the various issues
that burden us in this life or the life to come. It is almost strange to
hear Jesus tell us in John 15, that God's goal, wish, and desire for

our lives is for us to bear fruit of peace, joy, hope, and love. Because when we do, we bring God glory, which makes God happy. Which then means, when *you* are happy, that makes God happy. Imagine that, God is love. God loves you. God is happy when you are happy, so God came down here in the flesh to show us the Way to discover that kind of Abundant Life.

And the implications are enormous. The idea that Jesus was Truth means that there is an existence beyond our own, with its own myriad of implications regarding us having a soul, heaven, the afterlife, and so much more. The idea that Jesus was Truth also means that God is a loving Creator, who not only created the universe, but created you and me with a purpose - a purpose to be God's children, to be a part of God's family, to be loved by God and love Him in return, to share life with God, to experience abundance in life as God designed it to be, and so much more. The idea that Jesus is Truth also implies God has a place of residence, a home, a country separate from our world. In this, the purpose of this life is primarily about choosing whether we want to be with God in that life, in God's home forever, or not. And so much more.

It also implies that we are not alone. We are not cosmic orphans. We are not cosmic accidents, products of amino experiments gone awry with no rhyme or reason. No, we are children. *You* are a child of your heavenly Father, who created you with a purpose, a plan, a passion, and, again, so much more. Always, always, where "Jesus is Truth" is concerned, there is so much more. But again, that is not for our purposes here.

That being said, perhaps this broader view of things is a good place to conclude. For in the broad scope of things, in a galaxy with 100 billion stars, more stars than there are grains of sand on all the beaches of the earth, and in a universe with as many galaxies as there are stars in our 1 galaxy, it really can be depressing when we realize how truly small and insignificant we are in the big picture. Who are *you* to think you will ultimately add anything significant or meaningful to anything in this universe? Our world, our society, our culture offers many, many competing answers to that question, many alternative truths regarding the answers that are right and true. Even more, for most of us, we come into this world, and then are oppressed by the world into sincerely believing, and then confirming our biases, that we know the answer: I am nothing, and in the end, my life is futile. I will contribute nothing. Atheists agree. Agnostics agree. The other world religions agree, with hopes that you can achieve at least something on their terms to at least contribute a little.

But with Jesus, who was God's Truth living among us, well, it is a very different truth indeed. It is a very different story entirely. With Jesus, *you are something*. You are something and *someone* indeed, for you are God's beloved child. And if you will simply love Him back and follow where He leads, this "Jesus Truth" literally has the potential to transform your life forever, both in this life and the life to come.

Christian Logic 3
Christian Logic 2
Christian Logic 1

NOW ON AUDIBLE & EBOOK

www.thomaschilds.net

FB: DR. THOMAS CHILDS

ABOUT THE AUTHOR

Dr. Childs' education includes a Bachelors of Music in Jazz Studies, a Masters of Divinity, a Masters of Theology, a Doctorate of Ministry with an emphasis in Leadership, and studies abroad at the Goethe Institute in Mannheim, Germany.

Some of Dr. Childs' other accomplishments include touring with the Christian band TRUTH, as well as playing in the New Orleans Symphony, the New Orleans Saints Jazz Band, the Desire Brothers band, the Harmon Lights jazz band, and others. Dr. Childs was the first chair trumpet player in the state of Alabama All-State competition, first chair in the Southern United States Honor Band, and the Outstanding Music Major for Loyola Univ in 1993. Dr. Childs was the host operations director for the UMC General Conference in 2008. Dr. Childs also has been an adjunct faculty for Christian Leadership in the clinical pastoral education program at Harris Methodist Hospital, as well as teaching Christian Leadership at Texas Wesleyan University.

Made in the USA
Middletown, DE
06 June 2023